AMERICA the BEAUTIFUL
MINNESOTA

By R. Conrad Stein

Consultants

Stephen Sandell, Director, Humphrey Forum, Hubert H. Humphrey Institute of
Public Affairs, University of Minnesota

Rhoda R. Gilman, Senior Research Fellow, Minnesota Historical Society

Robert L. Hillerich, Ph.D., Bowling Green State University, Bowling Green, Ohio

 CHILDRENS PRESS®
CHICAGO

Spoonbridge and Cherry, a whimsical sculpture by Claes Oldenburg and
Coosje van Bruggen, stands in the Minneapolis Sculpture Garden.

Project Editor: Joan Downing
Associate Editor: Shari Joffe
Design Director: Margrit Fiddle
Typesetting: Graphic Connections, Inc.
Engraving: Liberty Photoengraving

Library of Congress Cataloging-in-Publication Data

Stein, R. Conrad.
    America the beautiful. Minnesota / by R. Conrad
Stein.
        p.   cm.
    Includes index.
    Summary: Discusses the geography, history,
people, government, economy, and recreation of
Minnesota.
        ISBN 0-516-00469-7
    1. Minnesota—Juvenile literature.
[1. Minnesota] I. Title.
F606.3.S74   1990   90-35384
977.6—dc20   CIP
                                           AC

Galtier Plaza, a shopping complex in St. Paul

TABLE OF CONTENTS

Chapter 1
WELCOME TO MINNESOTA

WELCOME TO MINNESOTA

Minnesota stands out as an American success story. Few other states enjoy its prosperity and high quality of life. Minnesota's fertile soil and humming factories rank it among the top ten states in both agricultural and industrial output. Its forward-thinking politics have generated such national leaders as Hubert Humphrey and Walter Mondale. Its school system is one of the nation's best. A land of forests and sparkling lakes, Minnesota's scenery is unrivaled.

The name *Minnesota* is derived from a Dakota Indian word meaning "sky-tinted water." Accordingly, one of Minnesota's nicknames is Land of Sky-Blue Waters. Certainly the association with water is appropriate. Lakes appear everywhere on the Minnesota map, giving rise to another of Minnesota's nicknames, Land of 10,000 Lakes.

Minnesota has also been nicknamed the North Star State, because Minnesota lies the farthest north of the lower forty-eight states; and the Bread and Butter State, for its wheat, flour mills, and dairy products. Its most famous nickname, however, came from an 1859 cartoon that portrayed a group of railroad promoters as gophers in top hats. They were trying to get state support for their line, and they succeeded. Hence, Minnesota was nicknamed the Gopher State.

Minnesota welcomes thousands of tourists, students, and new immigrants who come each year to capture the excitement, wonder, and opportunities the Gopher State has to offer. The state's golden past and a people and government unafraid of new ideas ensure a bright future for Minnesota.

Chapter 2
THE LAND

THE LAND

Minnesota lies in the upper Midwest portion of the United States. It shares borders with Iowa to the south, Wisconsin to the east, and North Dakota and South Dakota to the west. Its northern neighbors are the Canadian provinces of Ontario and Manitoba. Minnesota is considered a Great Lakes state. It has a long shoreline with Lake Superior, and the huge lake has had a profound influence on the state's development.

The Gopher State roughly resembles a rectangle with a great bite taken out of its eastern border. In the north, a small finger of its land juts into Canada. This northern peninsula, called the Northwest Angle, is the northernmost point of the lower forty-eight states.

Spreading over 84,402 square miles (218,601 square kilometers), Minnesota ranks twelfth in size among the states. It is the largest of all the midwestern states. St. Paul is the Gopher State's capital, and neighboring Minneapolis is the state's largest city.

LAND FORMS AND LAND USE

For hundreds of thousands of years, sheets of ice more than a mile (1.6 kilometers) thick crossed and recrossed the land now

Quartzite rock formations, a legacy of long-ago glaciers, punctuate the prairie at Blue Mounds State Park in southwestern Minnesota.

called Minnesota. Only the southeast corner of the state was untouched by glacial activity. The last of the great glaciers retreated from the upper Midwest about ten thousand years ago. Glacial activity left Minnesota with many hills and ridges, but no lofty mountains. Low areas created by the glaciers became lakes or marshes as they filled with water.

In geological terms, Minnesota has four distinct land regions: the Superior Upland, the Young Drift Plains, the Driftless Area, and the Dissected Till Plains. The Superior Upland, Minnesota's most rugged country, bulges out around Lake Superior and covers most of the northern half of the state. Its rough, rocky land contains most of Minnesota's iron-ore deposits. The wildest section of the Superior Upland lies between the Canadian border

Above: The St. Louis River near Duluth
Right: A farm near Chanhassen

and Lake Superior. This region, which on a map looks like an arrowhead, is called the Arrowhead Country. There, forests spread endlessly, and houses and other signs of civilization are few. Eagle Mountain, Minnesota's highest point, rises 2,301 feet (701 meters) near the town of Grand Marais in the Arrowhead Country.

The Young Drift Plains spread over the south of Minnesota and hug its western border with the Dakotas. As the glaciers melted in this region, they left fertile soil called *drift*. Minnesota's richest farmland, indeed some of the nation's best farmland, is in this region. The soil in southern Minnesota is so fertile that wheat farmers there grow fifty to sixty bushels an acre, while the national average is only thirty-four bushels an acre.

In the southwestern corner of the state lie the Dissected Till

Above: High Falls on the Pigeon River near Grand Portage

Plains. In this region, the glaciers deposited ripples of *till*, a mixture of sand, gravel, and clay. Rivers and streams here have dissected, or cut up, the land.

The Driftless Area—so named because glacial drift did not reach this area—is a small section of land in the southeast corner of the state. This region has limestone hills covered with hardwood forests. Its fine farmland is broken up by swift-flowing streams.

RIVERS AND LAKES

On license plates, Minnesota advertises itself as "Land of 10,000 Lakes." In reality, that boast is an understatement. Minnesota has 15,291 lakes, or 22,000 if ponds of less than 10 acres (4 hectares) are counted. The Minneapolis-St. Paul metropolitan area alone

The St. Croix River (above) is a chief branch of the Mississippi, which begins at Lake Itasca in north-central Minnesota (left).

contains thirty lakes. White Bear Lake, Lake of the Isles, and Lakes Minnetonka, Calhoun, and Harriet are a few of the lakes that provide recreation for the people of St. Paul and Minneapolis.

The state's largest lake is Red Lake, an hourglass-shaped body of water that is made up of Upper and Lower Red lakes and spreads over 430 square miles (1,114 square kilometers). Rainy Lake and the sprawling Lake of the Woods make up part of Minnesota's border with Canada. Lake Superior, the largest and deepest of North America's Great Lakes, forms Minnesota's northeastern border.

Minnesota has more than 25,000 miles (40,233 kilometers) of rivers and streams—enough to create one stream so long that it would wrap around the world at the equator. The mighty Mississippi has its source at Lake Itasca in north-central

Minnesota. As it flows out of the lake, the Mississippi is a creek so narrow and shallow that children can wade across it. To the southeast, the Mississippi River marks Minnesota's border with Wisconsin. The Minnesota River, which cuts across the southern third of the state, is a tributary of the Mississippi. Other major branches of the Mississippi include the Crow Wing, Rum, St. Croix, and Sauk rivers. The Red River of the North forms Minnesota's border with North Dakota. The St. Louis, a large river in the northeast, empties into Lake Superior.

Magnificent waterfalls are delightful features of the Gopher State. The tallest is Cascade Falls, which tumbles from a crevice as high as an eight-story building. Beautiful Minnehaha Falls, in Minneapolis, was made famous by Henry Wadsworth Longfellow's poem *The Song of Hiawatha*. The Falls of St. Anthony, also in Minneapolis, is the only natural waterfall on the Mississippi River.

PLANT AND ANIMAL LIFE

Thick forests once covered more than 70 percent of Minnesota. The unforested areas of Minnesota included the south-central and southwestern regions, which were covered by a tall grass prairie that extended all along the western edge of the state as far north as the Canadian border. Southeastern Minnesota and large parts of central Minnesota were largely prairie dotted with oak groves and other hardwoods. From present-day Mankato to St. Cloud spread an unbroken belt of forest so expansive that the pioneers called it the Big Woods. Logging and forest fires, however, reduced the magnificent trees to stumps, and today only patches of original forest remain.

Forests now cover about 35 percent of Minnesota. Minnesota's

Minnesota's varied landscape encompasses both forests (above) and grasslands (right).

woodlands, though made up of second-growth trees, are some of the grandest woodlands found anywhere in the nation. The 3-million-acre (1.2-million-hectare) Superior National Forest, which lies above Lake Superior, contains the state's most spectacular woods. The Chippewa National Forest and sixty-five state forests protect some of the remaining woodland. In the northern part of the state, balsam fir, pine, spruce, aspen, and white birch trees grow. Hardwood trees such as ash, black walnut, elm, maple, and oak grow in the southern part of the state.

In the spring, wildflowers explode across Minnesota. Asters, violets, and prairie phlox grow in the south and west. Lilies of the valley and wild blackberries, blueberries, and raspberries are

Black bears can be spotted in the woodlands of northern Minnesota.

common in the north. The beautiful pink and white lady's slipper is the state flower.

White-tailed deer are found everywhere in Minnesota. In the north, moose forage in the marshlands and black bears inhabit the woods. Minnesota is one of the few states where substantial numbers of timber wolves still roam free. At the town of Ely, which lies on the outskirts of the Superior National Forest, timber wolves can be heard howling at night. Gophers honeycomb the grasslands of the south with their burrows. Beavers and muskrats live in the state's rivers and ponds. The marshlands serve as nesting areas for flocks of ducks. In the rivers swim bass, northern pike, trout, muskie, walleye, and many other species of game fish.

A frigid winter day in Minneapolis

CLIMATE

Mention Minnesota to a group of Americans from other states and someone will surely wrap his arms around his chest, shiver, and say, "Brrrrr!" Undeniably, Minnesota has frigid winters. In the north, the average January temperature is 2 degrees Fahrenheit (minus 17 degrees Celsius). In the south, January temperatures average 15 degrees Fahrenheit (minus 9 degrees Celsius). The northern part of the state has been known to experience temperatures as low as minus 59 degrees Fahrenheit (minus 51 degrees Celsius). But Minnesotans have learned to enjoy the cold months. Tobogganing, skating, and ice fishing are popular sports. The snowmobile was invented in Minnesota. Minnesota has produced more professional and Olympic hockey players than any other state. Some communities hold winter festivals that include such outrageous activities as ice-cream-eating contests held on snowy cornfields.

The coldest city in this very cold state is International Falls, which lies on Rainy Lake along the Canadian border. The city is nationally famous because during January and February, it commonly records the lowest temperatures in the United States outside of Alaska. When the thermometer drops to 0 degrees Fahrenheit (minus 18 degrees Celsius) in Chicago, it is likely to be minus 40 degrees Fahrenheit (minus 40 degrees Celsius) in International Falls. Instead of moping about their arctic conditions, the people of International Falls have built a 22-foot- (7-meter-) tall thermometer outside the town so they can brag to the world about how cold it gets in their city.

By contrast, Minnesota summers are a delight. The average July temperature in the Twin Cities area is 74 degrees Fahrenheit (23 degrees Celsius). In the north, the average July temperature is 68 degrees Fahrenheit (20 degrees Celsius). Minnesota families spend the summer months out of doors, enjoying the state's woodlands and lakes. On occasion, however, Minnesota summers can be torrid. The highest temperature ever recorded in the state was 114 degrees Fahrenheit (46 degrees Celsius), at Beardsley on July 29, 1917, and at Moorhead on July 6, 1936.

As the many rivers and lakes attest, the state gets plenty of rainfall and snowfall. Spring rains accompanied by melting snow bring floods that plague many Minnesota communities. The Red River often overflows its banks, causing havoc in towns such as Moorhead, East Grand Forks, and other riverside communities. At the other extreme, the great nationwide drought of 1988 devastated many farms in the Gopher State. The drought caused the Minnehaha Falls to dry up for the first time in decades.

Chapter 3
THE PEOPLE

THE PEOPLE

*The Washington scene is fascinating. But, believe
me, the best place to be a politician is Minnesota.
This is a vast and exciting physical and political
environment. And the things that count here are
lakes, and rivers, and people.*
—Walter Mondale

POPULATION

The 1980 census counted 4,075,970 people living in Minnesota,
an increase of 7 percent over the 1970 census figure. The estimated
1986 population was 4,214,000. Minnesota ranks twenty-first
among the states in terms of population.

Almost seven of every ten Minnesotans live in cities and towns.
In order of population, the largest cities are Minneapolis, St. Paul,
Duluth, Bloomington, Rochester, and Edina. The fastest-growing
community is St. Cloud, whose population increased 9.7 percent
during the 1980s.

Southeastern Minnesota, which contains the Twin Cities of
Minneapolis and St. Paul, is the most heavily populated section of
the state. More than half the state's population lives in the
Minneapolis-St. Paul metropolitan area. The Twin Cities are the
political, economic, and cultural hub of the state. Other areas with
large populations are the iron-range towns of north-central
Minnesota; and the Duluth metropolitan area, an important
industrial and shipping center on Lake Superior.

Most of northern and western Minnesota is sparsely populated. The state's least-populated region is Koochiching County, in the far north near the Canadian border. Though Koochiching County is three times the size of Rhode Island, it has only 17,571 people. To lure new residents to this lovely but lonely county, local government leaders offered a unique land program. In 1989, the county announced that anyone willing to farm or otherwise develop 40-acre (16-hectare) plots of vacant land could have the land free of charge after a five-year period. Many thousands of people inquired about the land giveaway program.

WHO ARE THE MINNESOTANS?

Residents of other states may think of the average Minnesotan as being tall and blond and having a Swedish surname. Certainly, there are thousands of people in the state of Swedish heritage. The Minneapolis telephone book lists twenty-seven pages of Johnsons. But according to census figures, people of German heritage are the state's largest ethnic group, followed by Norwegians, with Swedes coming in only third. In fact, since its beginnings, the state has been home to people of nearly every racial and national group.

Native Americans (American Indians) were the original residents of Minnesota. White settlement was led by farmers from New York, Pennsylvania, and the New England states. Later, immigrants from Germany, Norway, Sweden, Denmark, England, and Ireland flowed in. The opening of iron-ore mines and the development of manufacturing brought newcomers from Finland, Lithuania, Poland, Slovenia, Serbia, Croatia, and Italy. During the two world wars, large numbers of blacks came to the state seeking industrial jobs. Hispanics and Asians are among the most recent immigrants to Minnesota. More than fifteen thousand Hmongs, a

Young Minnesotans participating in a *Cinco de Mayo* parade in St. Paul

tribal group from Laos in Southeast Asia, settled in Minnesota during the 1980s.

Today, nearly 97 percent of Minnesota residents are white. The 1980 census showed that about fifty-three thousand blacks and thirty-five thousand American Indians reside in the state. About one-quarter of Minnesota's American Indian population lives on the state's seven Ojibwa (or Chippewa) and four Dakota (or Sioux) reservations. The number of Asians and Hispanics in the state is small but growing.

Census figures also confirm that Minnesota is a healthy, safe, and prosperous place to live. Residents have an average life expectancy of 76.2 years, second among the states only to Hawaii. Compared to other states, Minnesota has a very low crime rate. Minnesota drivers have the lowest traffic deaths per mile of any state. Earnings of Minnesota workers are the fourteenth-highest in the nation.

RELIGION

More than 1.5 million Minnesotans are members of Protestant churches. Lutherans are the largest Protestant group, followed by Methodists, Presbyterians, and members of the United Church of Christ. About 1 million Minnesotans are Roman Catholic. Some thirty-five thousand residents are Jewish. The Amish, whose religious beliefs require them to shun automobiles and other modern trappings, operate farms in the southern third of the state. Amish horse-drawn buggies clip-clopping down roadways are a familiar sight in many rural communities.

POLITICS

Minnesota voters are among the most independent in the nation. Even the names of their political parties differ from the norm. The Minnesota Democratic party is officially called the Democratic-Farmer-Labor party (DFL), and the state's Republican party is known as the Independent-Republicans (IR).

Though nationally, Minnesota is perceived as a liberal, Democratic state, voters regularly cross party lines. In the 1984 presidential election, Minnesota was the only state to give the majority of its votes to Democratic candidate (and Minnesota native) Walter Mondale rather than to Republican Ronald Reagan. It was also one of the few states carried by Democratic presidential candidate Michael Dukakis in 1988. Yet during the 1980s, two of its most powerful political leaders were senators David Durenberger and Rudy Boschwitz, both Republicans.

Chapter 4
THE BEGINNINGS

THE BEGINNINGS

Come, it is time for you to depart.
We are going on a long journey.
—A death song sung by Ojibwa warriors in old Minnesota

THE FIRST MINNESOTANS

On a summer morning in 1932, a crew digging a roadbed through what once had been a glacial lake near Pelican Rapids uncovered a skeleton brittle with age. Archaeologists were summoned. Some estimated the skeleton to be eight thousand years old, while others claimed it was even older. Later research revealed that the skeleton was that of a young girl of about fifteen years of age. Hers are among the earliest human remains found in the upper Midwest. She is now known officially as Minnesota Woman.

The first human beings to enter what we now call Minnesota were the descendants of people who traveled from Asia to North America by crossing a land bridge that once existed in the Bering Sea. After a migration that lasted centuries, tiny bands settled on the banks of Lake Agassiz, a huge glacial lake that covered northern Minnesota thousands of years ago. Scientists believe Minnesota Woman died by drowning in a similar glacial lake, Lake Pelican.

The early Minnesotans probably hunted the exotic animals that once roamed the region—mammoths larger than elephants and giant beavers that weighed 500 pounds (227 kilograms). As the climate warmed, trees sprouted up and the huge Ice Age animals died out. The people then relied on elk and bison for food. They also fished and gathered wild rice, fruits, berries, and nuts.

About six thousand years ago, some of the early people of the Great Lakes region began to use copper. They found the mineral in its pure form along the shores of Lake Superior, and with skilled hands pounded it into tools and weapons. Many historians believe that the men and women of the Great Lakes were the first in the world to use copper.

About 500 B.C., during what scholars call the Woodland era, an amazing mound-building civilization spread into Minnesota. Earthen mounds built by ancient Indian workers were used as grave sites or as centers of worship. Archaeologists at one time identified more than ten thousand mounds in Minnesota. Some of them were effigy mounds in the shape of birds, buffaloes, bears, or snakes. Although many of these mounds disappeared as they were plowed under by farmers or damaged by curiosity seekers, some still remain. Today, families picnic beside the well-preserved pyramid-shaped mounds at Indian Mounds Park in St. Paul. One of the largest mounds still standing in the state is the Grand Mound, which rises on the Rainy River near the town of Laurel.

Between 300 B.C. and A.D. 1000, Indians in the southwestern corner of Minnesota began to mine a red stone called catlinite. From this stone they carved peace pipes known as *calumets*. The pipestone quarries became sacred ground for the Indians, and they traveled long distances to obtain the stone.

Evidence of ancient Indian civilizations is found throughout Minnesota. At a rocky ridge near the town of Jeffers are some two thousand pictures of animals, people, and religious symbols carved on the rocks by long-ago artists. Along the shores of

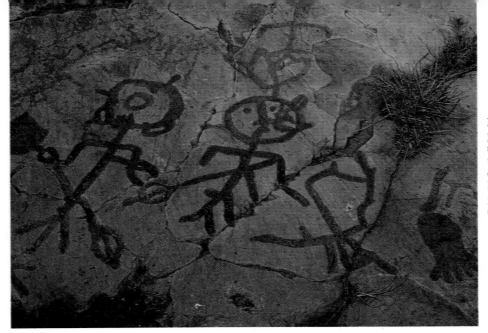

Minnesota's early people left behind such artifacts as these petroglyphs, carved on a rocky ledge near the present-day town of Jeffers.

Crooked Lake in the Arrowhead Country are hundreds of fading rock paintings, one clearly showing a sturgeon caught in a net.

THE DAKOTA AND THE OJIBWA

At the time Europeans first began exploring North America, the Dakota people dominated Minnesota. For centuries, the Dakota, also called the Santee Sioux, lived in the forests and grasslands of the upper Midwest. A large Dakota settlement stood on the banks of Mille Lacs Lake north of present-day Onamia. These people hunted, fished, and cultivated crops. Those living in the grasslands of the southwest stalked great herds of buffalo. Maple sugar, sapped from the trees, was considered a delicacy among forest dwellers. Dakota villagers often stayed on the grasslands in the summer and then moved to the forests in the winter. Their superbly designed, skin-covered tepees, which were easy to set up and take down, served as mobile homes.

In the late 1600s, a rival people, the Ojibwa, began pushing into Minnesota. The Ojibwa, also called the Chippewa, were an Algonquian-speaking tribe that came from the St. Lawrence River

Like the Plains Indians depicted in this painting by George Catlin (above), the Dakota who lived in southern Minnesota stalked great herds of buffalo. They were also skilled craftsmen, as this display at the Martin County Historical Society shows (right).

in the east. The European fur trade, which had begun in the east, triggered tribal warfare and sent many Indian people westward seeking new fur-trapping grounds. The Ojibwa were traders, trappers, and superb canoeists. They developed the lightweight birchbark canoe that was perfect for Minnesota's rivers and lakes. Wild rice, which grows in the state's many shallow lakes and marshes, was a major food source of both the Dakota and Ojibwa. Indians in the area began to use it about A.D. 500, and today it remains a favorite Minnesota specialty.

Music was important to the Ojibwa. In fact, they traveled as much to learn new songs as to trade goods. A line from one Ojibwa song illustrates their dedication to music: "The sky loves to hear me sing."

The meeting between the Ojibwa and the Dakota was tragic for both sides. The two peoples waged war on and off for almost a

Wild rice, shown here being gathered by Ojibwa Indians in the early 1900s, was a major food source of both the Dakota and Ojibwa of Minnesota.

century. By 1750, the Ojibwa controlled northern Minnesota, pushing the Dakota to the southwest part of the region.

Nevertheless, the Dakota and the Ojibwa had many religious beliefs in common. Both peoples believed in a single, all-powerful creator who headed a family of lesser gods and spirits. Ancestor worship and strong notions of life after death were common to both tribes. To the Ojibwa and the Dakota, nothing happened by chance. Scarcity of game animals during the icy winters was caused not by the cycles of nature but by some mischief-making spirit. Also, the Ojibwa and the Dakota faced a common rival for the land—the white Europeans who were penetrating the American interior in ever-increasing numbers.

FRENCH EXPLORERS, PRIESTS, AND VOYAGEURS

Who was the first white European to enter Minnesota? That question has triggered many arguments. The arguments stem from a Kensington farmer's 1898 discovery of a stone with curious

THE KENSINGTON RUNESTON

AUTHENTIC EVIDENCE THAT WHITE MEN VISITED DOUGLAS COUNTY IN 1362.

TRANSLATION ON FACE OF STONE READS:
"8 GOTHS AND 22 NORWEGIANS ON EXPLORATION—JOURNEY FROM VINLAND THROUGH THE WEST. WE HAD CAMP BY 2 SKERRIES (ROCKY ISLANDS) ONE DAYS-JOURNEY NORTH FROM THIS STONE. WE WERE (OUT) AND FISHED ONE DAY. AFTER WE CAME HOME FOUND 10 MEN RED WITH BLOOD AND DEAD. AV(M) M(ama) SAVE US FROM EVIL."

TRANSLATION ON EDGE OF STONE READS:
"HAVE 10 OF (OUR PARTY) BY THE SEA TO LOOK AFTER SHIP 14 DAYS JOURNEY FROM THIS ISLAND YEAR (1362)"

Some believe that the Kensington Runestone provides evidence that Vikings visited Minnesota as early as the 1300s.

writing on it. Experts determined that the writing chiseled on the stone was in runic, or old Norse, letters. Translated, it said, "Eight Goths and 22 Norwegians upon a journey of discovery from Vinland westward . . . . When we returned [to camp] we found ten men red with blood and dead." The writers then implored the Virgin Mary to "save us from evil." The inscription was dated "Year 1362."

Over the years, the Kensington Runestone has been pored over by archaeologists and linguists. Some claim it is genuine and stands as living proof that Norsemen, or Vikings, penetrated into midwestern America more than a hundred years before Columbus's voyage. Others say the stone is a hoax, cleverly written and planted in the farmer's field by some unknown prankster. However, those who reject the stone as false—pointing to the inaccuracy of some of the characters used—admit that whoever carved the writing had an impressive knowledge of the old Norse language. The arguments regarding the stone's authenticity rage to this day.

The first known Europeans to visit Minnesota were fur traders Pierre Radisson and Médard Chouart, Sieur des Groseilliers. Sometime between 1659 and 1661, the two Frenchmen entered Minnesota from Lake Superior, met with some Dakota, and returned to Montreal with canoes filled with furs. Some twenty years later, French explorer Daniel Greysolon, Sieur Duluth (also spelled Du Lhut), paddled his canoe to the western tip of Lake Superior and trekked inland. The modern city of Duluth now rises near the spot where the French trailblazer touched ground. Duluth thought that the northern rivers and lakes would lead to a sea passage to the Pacific. Although this elusive Northwest Passage did not exist, its quest hastened the European exploration of the Great Lakes region. While he was in the area, Duluth made friends with the Dakota and the Ojibwa. To protect the French fur trade, he urged the Dakota to make peace with the Ojibwa.

Following on the heels of the explorers were dark-robed priests who hoped to bring the word of Christ to the Indians. One was Father Louis Hennepin, who left the Illinois region and paddled north up the Mississippi in 1680. Hennepin and his companions were captured by a band of Dakota and taken to their camp at Mille Lacs. While being held prisoner, Hennepin became the first European to see the great falls of the Mississippi. Named the Falls of St. Anthony by Hennepin, they would later become the center of sprawling Minneapolis. Duluth heard about Hennepin's imprisonment and rushed to the Dakota camp to free him. The meeting between the explorer and the priest must have been one of high drama, as they were the only white men within hundreds of miles.

Sailing under the French banner, a colorful band of fortune

A nineteenth-century painting of French voyageurs on Lake Superior in the 1700s

hunters called *voyageurs* (travelers) came to the Great Lakes in the early 1700s. The voyageurs' job was to transport the goods of the fur trade. Some of these men, known as "porkeaters," brought goods in 48-foot- (15-meter-) long freight canoes from Montreal to such inland depots as Grand Portage and Mackinac. They then returned to Montreal loaded with furs from the scattered winter posts. The round-trip journey, which covered some 3,000 miles (4,828 kilometers), took the voyageurs through rivers and over lakes subject to treacherous storms. Other voyageurs, known as "winterers," were assigned to the various posts. Using smaller canoes, they carried the goods into the back country and stayed there through the winter.

The fur trade brought changes to the Indian way of life. Once independent farmers and hunters, the Indians became hired trappers for the French. One beaver skin bought an Indian trapper two iron chisels. Two skins could be traded for a good-sized kettle. Twelve beaver pelts bought the ultimate prize—a European gun. The Ojibwa, who were skilled traders, were the first Indian group in Minnesota to acquire guns. So armed, they were able to force many Dakota bands to move west.

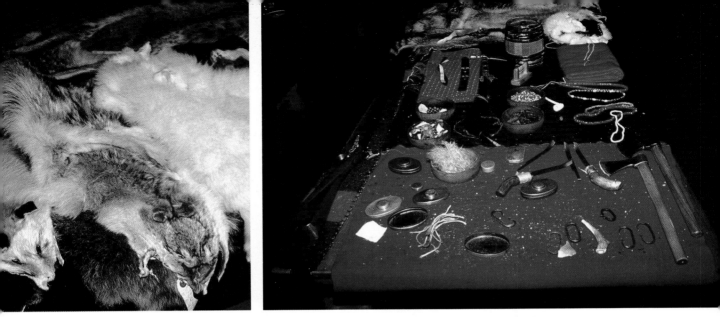

Furs (left) and other goods (right) traded in the Minnesota region during the 1700s are displayed at Grand Portage National Monument.

THE BRITISH PERIOD

In Europe in the 1700s, beaver pelts and other furs were literally worth their weight in gold. During this time, France and England fought a series of wars that spilled over into their American holdings. In America, the wars, known as the French and Indian Wars, were fought partly for control over the fur trade. The outcome of the wars affected European land claims in the New World. In 1763, the last of the conflicts ended in a British victory. France was forced to cede Canada, its Great Lakes land holdings, and all the land east of the Mississippi River, including northern Minnesota, to Britain. To Spain, France ceded the region west of the Mississippi River, which included western Minnesota.

To control the fur trade, the British built forts at key river junctions. There, soldiers could stop foreign fur-trading boats and allow only boats chartered by British companies to pass. One of the largest British firms operating on the Great Lakes was the North West Company, which was headquartered in Grand Portage.

The change from French to British control over the Great Lakes region infuriated the Indians. The French had always lived as brothers with the Indian people. The British, on the other hand, treated the Indians as a conquered race. Under the Ottawa leader Pontiac, Great Lakes Indians rebelled and attacked British forts in 1763. Eight forts fell to Indian warriors. But in the end, the Indians were forced to accept British rule.

The British period in the Great Lakes lasted about fifty years. A highlight of the British experience was the exploration effort of Jonathan Carver, a Massachusetts colonist who made an adventurous trip through the Wisconsin and Minnesota forests in 1766. Although Carver made no new discoveries, his book about Indian life and customs in the region was the first one in English. It became popular in England and in the eastern colonies and interested more people in Minnesota.

No fighting took place on Minnesota soil during the American Revolutionary War, and the fur trade at Grand Portage continued as briskly as ever. At the peace conference that ended the war, Britain gave the United States all its land south of the Great Lakes and east of the Mississippi River, including eastern Minnesota. Because the young nation was unable to enforce its claims in northern Minnesota, the British continued to control the fur trade and avoided paying the United States duties on the furs.

In 1800, Napoleon, the emperor of France, forced Spain to return the Louisiana region to France. Three years later, Napoleon sold it to the United States. Through this massive acquisition of land, the rest of Minnesota became part of the United States. The British refused to give up their trading rights, however. American victories over Britain in the Great Lakes region during the War of 1812 finally put Minnesota firmly under United States control.

Fort Snelling, built in 1819, was for a time the northernmost outpost of the Northwest Territory.

THE AMERICAN DAWN

The first American explorer to enter Minnesota was Lieutenant Zebulon Pike. President Thomas Jefferson approved Pike's expedition to survey the new lands of the Northwest. Pike and twenty soldiers reached the confluence of the Mississippi and Minnesota rivers in the fall of 1805. On what is today Pike Island, he raised what was probably the first American flag to fly over Minnesota soil. Pike then met with Dakota chiefs and bought a parcel of land at the vital river junction. Some fourteen years later, Colonel Josiah Snelling was sent to the river site to oversee the building of a fort. Named Fort Snelling in 1825, it became the finest fort in the northwestern wilderness.

Fort Snelling had a host of functions. In its early days, it served as a stopover for American explorers Lewis Cass, Stephen Long, and Henry Schoolcraft. In 1820, Cass explored the Mississippi River and Lake Superior areas. Long explored the southern

Today, costumed guides help re-create life at Fort Snelling in the 1820s.

Mississippi Valley in Minnesota and the Minnesota and Red River valleys in 1823. In 1832, Schoolcraft, guided by an Ojibwa named Ozawindib, found and mapped the source of the Mississippi River, at a lake that he named Itasca.

In 1823, Fort Snelling saluted the *Virginia*, the first Mississippi River steamboat to reach the northern outpost from St. Louis. From 1821 to 1840, the fort's walls offered protection for an early group of settlers known as the Selkirkers. Eventually, some of the Selkirk colonists helped to found St. Paul.

Fort Snelling also anchored the region's fur trade. The tiny village of Mendota, which rose on the east bank of the Mississippi opposite Fort Snelling, was the most important trading center in the area. One well-known trader in the region was a black man named Pierre Bonga, who traded in the Red River Valley. His son, George Bonga, served as an Indian-language interpreter for explorer Lewis Cass. George Bonga later opened a lucrative fur-trading office at Leech Lake.

Two well-known figures during Minnesota's territorial days were fur trader George Bonga (left) and politician Alexander Ramsey (right).

Initially, the United States called the huge land mass around the Great Lakes the Northwest Territory. As settlers streamed in, Congress carved smaller territories out of this sprawling region. Territorial borders shifted readily. At various times, Minnesota was part of Michigan Territory, Wisconsin Territory, and Iowa Territory.

In March 1849, Congress created the Minnesota Territory. Its boundaries were very similar to those of the present state. Alexander Ramsey, a young lawyer from Pennsylvania, became the first territorial governor. Ramsey eventually served Minnesota as state governor and as a United States senator. St. Paul was chosen as the territorial capital. Several names were suggested for the new territory, including Chippewa, Itasca, Jackson, and Washington. Finally, all parties agreed upon Minnesota, the colorful Dakota word meaning "sky-tinted water."

Chapter 5
THE PIONEER ERA

THE PIONEER ERA

Here [in Minnesota] people will find an unqualified,
healthy climate, fertile and well drained lands. . . .
Thrifty towns will arise. . . . These hills resound
with the voices of schoolchildren, and churches shall
mark the moral progress of the land.
—From a newspaper called the *Minnesota Pioneer*,
published in 1849

TERRITORIAL DAYS

In 1850, the territory of Minnesota had about 4,000 non-Indian residents; seven years later, that figure had soared to 150,000. Improved transportation and the acquisition of Indian land accounted for the spectacular growth.

Two treaties signed by Dakota chiefs in 1851 ceded 28 million acres (11 million hectares) of southern Minnesota land to the United States government. That land included some of the nation's best farmland. Another treaty, arranged with the Ojibwa in 1854, relinquished that tribe's claim to much of the rich timberland of northern Minnesota. In return, the Indians received a small cash payment—about twelve and a half cents per acre of land—and promises of more money and services in the future. The government set up reservations on which the Indians were to live. In the years to come, Indian resentment over the treaties led to a bloody war.

Transportation improved tremendously when Mississippi River steamboats began a regular run from the railroad center of Rock Island, Illinois, to St. Paul. The passage of steamboats gave the

An authentic
pioneer sod house
at the Nobles County
Pioneer Village
in Worthington

people of the territory some of their most exciting moments. In tiny upper Mississippi towns such as Winona, Wabasha, Red Wing, Frontenac, and Hastings, the entire population poured out onto the wharves to cheer and wave as the great paddle-wheel boats lumbered by. During the summer months, two riverboats a day, carrying some four hundred people each, completed the three-day trip from Galena to St. Paul.

Most of the early settlers of the Minnesota Territory came from the eastern states. These "Yankees" were experienced pioneers who had already helped to develop Ohio, northern Illinois, Michigan, and Wisconsin. The towns they built looked strikingly similar to those they left behind. The tiny village of Marine-on-

An 1880 photograph of Minnesota's first commercial flour mill, which opened in 1854 at the Falls of St. Anthony

St. Croix stands today as a lovely example of New England architecture transplanted to the Midwest.

During the territorial years, the lumber industry grew to provide the materials needed to build homes and commercial buildings in the new towns. Timber cutting began in the St. Croix Valley on the state's eastern border and quickly moved into the southern edge of the pine forests along the Mississippi in central Minnesota. Sawmills at Stillwater, a logging center on the St. Croix River, cut the logs into lumber.

Though logging was the biggest industry, agriculture and milling also thrived. Farmers flocked to southern Minnesota, where they bought land from the federal government at a cost of $1.25 per acre ($3.08 per hectare). By 1856, more than 1 million acres (0.4 million hectares) had been sold. Farming villages such as Mankato and New Ulm appeared along the Minnesota River.

Wheat from Minnesota's farms helped establish the milling industry. In 1854, Minnesota's first commercial flour mill opened at the Falls of St. Anthony. More mills opened on other rivers and streams, and by 1858, some eighty-five mills hummed in Minnesota.

Stillwater, the largest town in the Minnesota Territory, was famed and feared for the drunken parties thrown by lumberjacks. St. Paul, the territory's capital, was also a brawling town. Early in its history, St. Paul was called Pig's Eye after a one-eyed whiskey seller who set up shop at present-day Jackson Street and the riverbank. Near St. Paul was the community of St. Anthony, which grew up on the east side of the waterfall of the same name. In 1872, St. Anthony merged with and took the name of a community that had developed on the west side of the falls—Minneapolis.

STATEHOOD

By 1856, the Minnesota Territory held more than the sixty thousand settlers required to become a state. However, because Minnesota would be admitted as a free, or nonslave, state, the southerners in Congress refused to accept Minnesota until Kansas, projected as a proslavery state, was admitted.

While arguments continued in Washington, D.C., the settlers of Minnesota drafted a constitution and elected a legislature. In a raucous and mud-slinging campaign, merchant and fur trader Henry Sibley defeated Alexander Ramsey to become the first governor. Finally, on May 11, 1858, Congress admitted Minnesota into the Union as the thirty-second state.

With statehood came grave responsibilities. In April 1861, southern ships fired upon Fort Sumter, and the United States plunged into the bloody Civil War. Governor Alexander Ramsey, who had been elected in 1859, happened to be in Washington, D.C., when Fort Sumter was bombarded. As soon as he heard the news, Ramsey rushed to the War Department and offered the Union a thousand men from the Minnesota militia. Minnesota thus became the first northern state to answer the Union's call for fighting men.

During the war years, Minnesota's troops gained a reputation for bravery, but they suffered shocking casualties. In a single charge at Gettysburg, eight of every ten soldiers in the First Minnesota Regiment were either killed or wounded. More than twenty thousand Minnesota men served in the Civil War, and some twenty-five hundred never returned home.

THE DAKOTA WAR

While Civil War battles raged hundreds of miles from Minnesota, serious trouble brewed within the state's borders. For years, the Dakota people had seethed while seeing their land invaded and occupied by whites. Worse yet, because of Civil War supply problems, in 1862, the United States government failed to deliver money, food, and other goods that had been promised by treaty to the Indians. In August 1862, an incident occurred that triggered the Dakota War. A hunting party of four Dakota tribesmen got into an argument with some settlers in the central Minnesota River Valley. A fight broke out, and the Dakota men killed five settlers—three men and two women. People in the frontier communities were furious about the murders.

In the Dakota camp, Chief Little Crow urged the tribe to make peace with the white settlers. Little Crow had been to Washington, D.C., and knew the white man's power and superior numbers. But younger leaders argued that since thousands of Minnesota

A painting depicting Indians attacking the town of New Ulm during the Dakota War

soldiers were fighting on Civil War battlefronts, it was an ideal time to drive the settlers out of Dakota land. The voices urging war won the tribal debates, and fifteen hundred Dakota braves took to the warpath.

The Dakota burned the Indian agency building near the present-day city of Redwood Falls. From there they advanced on nearby Fort Ridgely. A reluctant Chief Little Crow commanded the war party. Even though his pleas for peace had gone unheard, he was determined to fight and die with his tribe. While Little Crow led his men into battle against soldiers, renegade Dakota bands scoured the countryside, murdering women and children and looting settlements. Battles that pitted settlers against Indians raged up and down the Minnesota River. Fighting at New Ulm spread to the streets, the alleys, and the cowsheds, but the settlers held the town.

Swedish immigrants (above) were among those who flocked to Minnesota after The Homestead Act was passed in 1862.

The end came for the Dakota in September 1862, when troops commanded by former governor Henry Sibley forced them to surrender. More than four hundred whites had been killed during the Dakota War, and the settlers hungered for revenge. Sibley ordered hasty trials for the defeated warriors, and 306 Dakota tribesmen were condemned to death by hanging. A mass execution of such magnitude shocked American President Abraham Lincoln. Believing the trials had been unfair, Lincoln commuted the death sentences for all but thirty-nine of the Dakota. The sentences were carried out on December 26, 1862, in the town of Mankato. The hanging of thirty-eight men (one man's death sentence was reprieved at the last moment) was perhaps the largest one-day execution in the nation's history.

The Dakota War spelled the doom of Indian power in Minnesota. In spite of the fact that not all of the Dakota had joined the war, all were later punished by forced removal and loss of their treaty rights. After the conflict, most of the Dakota were deported to the Missouri Valley, and their reservation land was opened to white settlers.

THE FLOOD OF IMMIGRANTS

"Free land! Free land!" These words celebrated the passage of the revolutionary Homestead Act of 1862. The act, which was introduced in Congress by Representative Cyrus Aldrich of Minnesota, gave 160 acres (65 hectares) of land free to any head of a family who agreed to develop it over a five-year period. An applicant for the land did not even have to be a citizen of the United States. In just three years, more than 1 million acres (0.4 million hectares) of Minnesota farmland had been given away to a small army of homesteaders. This influx caused the population of Minnesota to jump to nearly five hundred thousand by 1870.

Northern Europeans led the flood of homesteaders. To encourage immigrants, the state printed pamphlets in German, Swedish, and Norwegian extolling the riches of Minnesota. The pamphlets were distributed in Europe and to immigrants climbing off ships in New York City. The railroads also joined the campaign to lure Europeans to Minnesota. Railroad companies owned vast tracts of land that they were willing to divide into farm-sized parcels and sell cheaply to European farmers. Many Irish immigrants took advantage of the railroads' offers.

By 1880, one-third of the state's population was foreign-born, and a far greater percentage had parents who had been born in the Old World. Germans were the first Europeans to come in large numbers. New Ulm, Winona, Sauk Rapids, and St. Cloud had large German communities. St. Paul was a center for Irish and German traders and shopkeepers. The Swedes fell under Minnesota's spell because the countless lakes reminded them of southern Sweden. The towns of Almelund, Kost, Lindstrom, and Stark were named after Swedish pioneers. Chisago and Isanti counties, north of St. Paul, became known as Swedeland, U.S.A. Immigrants from Norway settled in the southern and western parts of the state. Norwegian intellectual leaders founded St. Olaf College in Northfield and Concordia College in Moorhead.

THE WORLD OF FRONTIER AGRICULTURE

Some 60 percent of frontier Minnesota's farmland was devoted to wheat. Wheat farmers in the 1860s had to cut their stalks, allow them to dry, and then beat the stalks with sticks to remove the grain. By the 1870s, horse-driven threshing machines eased some of the work of harvesting.

Struggling farmers in Minnesota were forever at the mercy of nature's whims. A great blizzard howled over the northern part of the state in 1873, burying houses and barns. At least seventy people and countless cows and horses were killed under the driving snow. In 1876, swarms of grasshoppers, so thick that they blotted out the light of the sun, reduced the wheat to stubble. The insects were so ravenous that they even devoured clothing hanging on the line to dry.

Despite the hard work and many setbacks, Minnesota farm families developed a special pride in their land. For many homesteaders—especially the Europeans—this was the first land they had ever owned. One German immigrant, who owned a farm near Stillwater, summed up his feelings for his newfound way of life in a letter home: "If a man there [in Germany] has more

Above: A Minnesota State Grange meeting at Northfield in 1875
Right: Ignatius Donnelly, a Minnesota politician who championed
the cause of the farmer

money than you, you have to bow and scrape and take off your
hat to him. That is certainly not true here [in Minnesota]. Here a
man who is healthy and works hard can get along better than a
rich man in our village in Germany.''

The most explosive political issue on the agricultural frontier
was the power of the railroad companies. While the railroads
aided the farmer by opening up new markets, they also cut into
farm profits by charging sky-high rates to ship harvested goods to
the cities. In the 1860s, a Minnesotan named Oliver Kelley
founded a cooperative organization to help farmers that was
popularly called the Grange. By 1869, forty Grange organizations
were active in Minnesota, and nine chapters met in other states.
Under the leadership of Ignatius Donnelly, another popular leader
among the state's small farmers, Minnesota's Grange groups
pressured state legislatures and the United States Congress to
regulate the freight rates that railroads charged farmers. An
activist since territorial days, Donnelly served Minnesota as

James J. Hill (standing on wheel) built the Great Northern Railway, which opened trade between Minnesota and the Northwest.

lieutenant governor, as a state legislator, and as a United States representative. In addition to holding government offices, Donnelly was a newspaper editor and a best-selling author.

THE RISE OF INDUSTRY

The first railroad in Minnesota was completed in 1862 and ran 10 miles (16 kilometers) from St. Paul to St. Anthony. Within five years, newly laid tracks linked St. Paul with Austin, Anoka, and the Red River Valley community of Breckenridge. By 1872, more than 2,000 miles (3,219 kilometers) of railroad track crisscrossed Minnesota. The state's greatest railroad builder was James J. Hill. Arriving in St. Paul at age eighteen, Hill worked as a shipping clerk and a warehouse laborer before entering the railroad business. In 1878, he gained control of the bankrupt St. Paul and Pacific Railroad Company. Out of that troubled company, Hill built the Great Northern Railway, which opened trade between Minnesota and the burgeoning states of Oregon and Washington.

Minnesota's lumbering industry benefited from the railroads in several ways. Not only did the railroads make it easier to transport Minnesota pine to other parts of the country, but the very construction of the railroads required large quantities of lumber. Thus, the lumbering business entered a new and relentlessly efficient stage as a small army of lumberjacks mowed down Minnesota's remaining forests in the north and in the Arrowhead region. In its heyday, Minnesota's lumber industry employed forty thousand men. The leading lumberman was Frederick Weyerhaeuser, who made St. Paul the headquarters for his company. By the time he died in 1914, Weyerhaeuser owned a timber empire that stretched from the Atlantic to the Pacific and from Canada to Mexico. For Minnesota, the sad result of the lumbering frenzy was the almost complete destruction of its once-magnificent forests.

Flour milling triggered Minnesota's growth more than any single industry. Minnesota's many rushing rivers generated power to operate flour mills. By 1870, more than five hundred water-driven flour mills operated in the state's wheat-growing regions. The winning combination of wheat and waterpower made Minnesota the nation's leading flour producer by 1882, and Minneapolis soon became known as the "Mill City."

Two prosperous Minneapolis mill owners were Cadwallader Washburn and Charles Pillsbury. Washburn developed a way of milling Minnesota's spring wheat so that its flour was as white as the flour of the western states' winter wheat. Washburn eventually formed the corporate giant known as General Mills. Pillsbury started the company that still bears his name. Both of their families played important roles in Minnesota's development.

Pillsbury's uncle, John S. Pillsbury, was governor of Minnesota from 1876 to 1882 and aided in the development of the University of Minnesota. Washburn's brothers Elihu and William served in Congress.

As early as Civil War times, gold prospectors uncovered rich iron-ore deposits near Vermilion Lake in northeast Minnesota. The first ore was shipped from the Vermilion Range in 1884. But it took the dogged determination of Leonidas Merritt and his six brothers to make the real find. After patient exploring and digging, the Merritt brothers finally struck a fabulously rich deposit of iron ore at the Mesabi Range in 1890. In time, iron-ore mines operated on three northeast Minnesota iron-ore ranges: the Vermilion, the Mesabi, and the Cuyuna. Production from the Mesabi Range alone was enough to make Minnesota the nation's leading provider of iron ore. Mining transformed life in the once-undeveloped northeast as villages such as Eveleth, Hibbing, Crosby, Ironton, Virginia, Babbitt, and Chisholm suddenly boomed.

No city benefited more from the iron-ore prosperity than the Lake Superior port of Duluth. By the 1890s, Duluth's docks were shipping 12 million short tons (11 million metric tons) of ore a year. The city was the fifth-busiest seaport in the nation, despite the fact it was more than 2,000 miles (3,219 kilometers) from the Atlantic Ocean. In addition to iron ore, Duluth shipped lumber, coal, and Minnesota flour. Duluth also became a shipbuilding center when an enterprising resident, Alexander McDougall, designed and built a new type of flat-bottomed iron-ore carrier. By the late 1890s, McDougall's ships were the workhorses of the iron-ore trade.

Tragedy struck Minnesota's forestland when a raging fire broke out near Hinckley in September 1894. Fueled by waste material

In 1894, a huge forest fire devastated a large part of eastern Minnesota and wiped out several towns, including Hinckley.

and rotting logs left by lumber companies, the fire spread over five counties and reduced several communities to ashes. More than four hundred people lost their lives because of the blaze. The Great Hinckley Fire was neither the first nor the last forest fire to devastate Minnesota, but it had a positive result. After the fire, Christopher Andrews, a St. Cloud resident, became the state's forest commissioner. Under Andrews, long overdue efforts were launched to preserve Minnesota's remaining forests.

Mining on the iron range and the development of manufacturing in Minneapolis and St. Paul brought a new wave of immigrants to Minnesota. This time, many of the newcomers came from eastern and southern Europe. The agricultural frontier had long been closed, so the immigrants took jobs in the mines and in city factories. Between 1890 and 1920, mining towns became filled with Italians, Hungarians, Poles, and Yugoslavians. Many eastern and southern Europeans also settled in the Twin Cities region, where meat-packing plants and food-processing firms offered employment.

A vigorous Minnesota faced the twentieth century. With the state's economy firmly based in agriculture and industry and with a population that topped 1.7 million in 1900, the people looked to the future with confidence.

Chapter 6

TWENTIETH-CENTURY MINNESOTA

TWENTIETH-CENTURY MINNESOTA

Minnesota is a special political place. It has a
conservative base, primarily built around the old Yankees
who dominated business and finance in the cities, the
rural German Catholic population, and large elements of
Scandinavians both urban and rural. But from that solid
and rocky base have blossomed wild flowers of political,
social, and economic radicalism.
—Hubert H. Humphrey

MINNESOTA ENTERPRISES

William W. Mayo was a highly respected doctor who practiced in Rochester. He was among the first physicians in Minnesota to use a microscope to diagnose diseases. His two sons, William J. and Charles, became doctors and assisted their father. A terrible tornado leveled Rochester in 1883, and the Mayos treated hundreds of injured townspeople. The tornado dramatized the need for a community hospital, and in 1889, St. Mary's Hospital was founded. That year, the Mayos formed a clinic at the hospital. Today, the Mayo Clinic treats a quarter of a million patients a year and is one of the most famous medical facilities in the world.

The Mayo Clinic is just one example of Minnesota enterprises that developed near the turn of the century. These enterprises extended to community organizations and to state politics.

During the 1890s and early 1900s, farmers believed they were being cheated by the railroads and by agricultural firms such as grain-elevator companies and flour mills. To achieve independence from these big agricultural businesses, rural Minnesotans pooled money to buy their own grain elevators,

The Mayo Clinic (right), one of the world's finest medical centers, was started in 1889 by the Mayo family (above), which included William W. Mayo (at center) and his sons Charles and William, Jr.

creameries, and storage facilities. By 1922, some forty-five hundred cooperative organizations had been organized by Gopher State farmers. These co-ops made it possible for farmers to buy and sell goods at reasonable prices. The farm co-ops often backed political candidates and eventually acquired a strong voice in state government.

In 1918, an organization called the Farmer's Nonpartisan League supported Congressman Charles A. Lindbergh, Sr., in the primary campaign for governor against the incumbent Joseph A. A. Burnquist. Lindbergh favored programs that called for state ownership of grain elevators and flour mills. But Lindbergh had been a staunch opponent of the entrance of America into World War I. Running for governor during the peak of American involvement in the war, Lindbergh was called unpatriotic, a coward, and a traitor. Lindbergh lost by a wide margin. Arthur C.

A crowd listening to a Farmer's Nonpartisan League speaker in 1918

Townley, who had founded the Farmer's Nonpartisan League, hastily put together the Minnesota Farmer-Labor party, and ran David H. Evans as its candidate for governor in the general election. Evans lost, but came in ahead of the Democratic candidate. From that day forward, state politicians were forced to heed the voice of organized farmers.

PROSPERITY AND HARD TIMES

Though the farmers managed to flex their political muscle, they were unable to win elections against the Republican party, which had long dominated the state. Clearly, the farmers had to broaden their appeal. In 1922, the Farmer-Labor party was officially organized. It was designed to appeal to the small farmer as well as to the big-city factory worker. The new party scored an early success in 1922, when Farmer-Labor candidate Henrik Shipstead was elected to the United States Senate over the popular Republican Senator Frank Kellogg.

Despite this defeat, Kellogg commanded world headlines when, in 1925, he became United States secretary of state under President Calvin Coolidge. In 1928, he negotiated the historic Kellogg-Briand Pact with French Foreign Minister Aristide Briand. This forward-looking treaty, which was eventually signed by sixty-two nations, denounced war as a means of foreign policy. For his efforts, Kellogg won the 1929 Nobel Peace Prize.

The greatest hero of the 1920s was the shy aviator Charles Lindbergh, Jr., the son of Congressman Charles Lindbergh. In May 1927, Lindbergh's flimsy single-engine airplane, the *Spirit of St. Louis*, rumbled off a field in New York State and nosed over the Atlantic Ocean. Its destination was Paris, France—3,600 miles (5,793 kilometers) away. ''Looking ahead at the unbroken horizon and the limitless expanse of water, I'm struck by my arrogance in attempting such a flight,'' Lindbergh later wrote. Fighting bone-numbing fatigue and Atlantic ice storms, Lindbergh landed in Paris after a thirty-three-hour flight. It was the first solo transatlantic flight in history. For years to come, ''Lucky Lindy's'' fame exceeded that of the king of England and the president of the United States.

During the 1920s, many Minnesotans shared in the prosperity that swept the nation. Milk production increased, and the number of cooperatives grew. Minneapolis and St. Paul experienced a building boom as tall office and bank buildings dotted their skylines. However, the prosperous 1920s ended with the stock market crash of 1929, which ushered in the nation's Great Depression. By 1932, 70 percent of the state's iron-ore miners had lost their jobs. In the Twin Cities, one of every three factory workers was laid off. Prices for farm goods tumbled. Wheat

Minnesotan Charles Lindbergh, Jr., (right) made the world's first solo transatlantic flight. His father, Charles, Sr., (left, with young Charles), was a prominent Minnesota politician.

dropped from $1.20 a bushel in 1929 to 50¢ a bushel in 1932. Minnesota dairy farmers saw their income reduced to one-quarter of pre-crash levels.

Labor unrest swept the state. In what was the nation's first large-scale "sit-down" strike, workers at a Hormel meat-packing plant in Austin reported to their jobs, then sat down and refused to work. The state's most violent strike occurred in 1934, when hundreds of truck drivers who supplied the Twin Cities with food walked off their jobs. More than twenty thousand people formed a citizens' army to protect nonstriking truck drivers from the strikers. Fights broke out, leaving two people dead and dozens injured. Governor Floyd Olson, who had been elected as the first Farmer-Labor governor in 1930, called out the state militia to restore order.

During the depression years, the vast majority of Minnesotans shunned acts of violence and used their votes to promote change.

In May 1934, violence erupted between striking Twin Cities truck drivers and a citizens' army that had formed to protect nonstriking truckers.

In 1932, Minnesotans, led by Governor Olson, cast a majority of their ballots for Franklin Delano Roosevelt, marking the first time ever that the state was carried by a Democratic presidential candidate. The popularity of the Farmer-Labor party soared, and Olson was reelected governor in 1934. After the 1936 election, the state's governor, two United States senators, and the majority of the representatives in the state legislature were all Farmer-Labor party members.

WARTIME MINNESOTA

The bombs that rained down on Pearl Harbor on December 7, 1941, snapped the United States and Minnesota out of the Great Depression. The state's lumber and mining industries produced raw materials for the war effort. During the war years, 60 percent of American iron ore came from the Gopher State. Before the war, the Minnesota Mining and Manufacturing Company (also known as the 3M Company) had marketed a brand of cellophane tape

popularly called Scotch tape. Turning to war production, the
3M Company made clear tape that protected the windshields
of fighter planes. The Minneapolis-Honeywell Company
manufactured delicate aircraft parts. The Owatonna Tool
Company churned out heavy wrenches used by navy ships.
Landlocked Minnesota was even a major shipbuilder; yards in
Duluth and in the Minnesota River town of Savage assembled
oceangoing oil tankers.

More than three hundred thousand Minnesotans served in the
armed forces during World War II. Some six thousand lost their
lives in the conflict. One notable Minnesota serviceman was
Governor Harold Stassen, who resigned from office in 1943 to
become an officer in the navy.

An important political development occurred during the war
years when the state Farmer-Labor party merged with the state
Democratic party. Allies for many years, the two groups formed
the Democratic-Farmer-Labor party (DFL) in 1944. One of the
leading figures orchestrating the merger was young Minneapolis
politician Hubert H. Humphrey.

THE POSTWAR PERIOD

The years following World War II saw sweeping changes in the
Gopher State. In the late 1940s, Governor Luther W. Youngdahl
oversaw the building of highways, bridges, and hospitals.
Youngdahl also created the Youth Conservation Commission,
which put juvenile lawbreakers to work on useful projects.

The 1950 census revealed that the majority of Minnesotans were
living in urban areas. This was significant because just two
generations earlier, nine out of ten Minnesota residents had lived
on farms. The construction of new factories and roadways in the

Twin Cities suburbs accounted for much of the urban growth. One suburban milestone was the 1956 completion of Southdale, the nation's first fully enclosed shopping mall.

The state's iron-ore industry experienced reversals as well as a triumph in the postwar period. In the early 1950s, Minnesota's ranges began to run out of high-grade iron ore. Northern Minnesota, however, was still rich in a low-grade iron ore called taconite. Years earlier, Edward W. Davis, a University of Minnesota engineer, had begun experiments designed to make taconite usable in the nation's blast furnaces. Davis's efforts, funded largely by the university, were successful. By the time the high-grade iron ore was almost depleted, taconite took its place. Voters later approved the "taconite amendment," which limited state taxes on taconite mining operations.

The postwar years saw the rise of Minnesota's remarkable political personalities. Navy veteran and former governor Harold Stassen became a popular Republican party figure. Stassen was a strong candidate for the Republican presidential nomination in 1948, but lost to Thomas E. Dewey. He served the Eisenhower administration in positions dealing with foreign affairs. In 1948, Hubert Humphrey rose from mayor of Minneapolis to the United States Senate as the DFL's candidate. Humphrey was one of America's strongest civil-rights activists and led the fight in the Senate to end racial segregation. Also in 1948, college professor Eugene McCarthy ran successfully as a DFL candidate for the United States House of Representatives. He held that office until 1959, when he joined Humphrey in the Senate. The Democratic Convention of 1960, which chose John F. Kennedy as its candidate, was in part a celebration of Minnesota's political talent. Humphrey, McCarthy, and Governor Orville Freeman all played important roles in the convention process.

TODAY'S MINNESOTA

The closest race for governor in the state's history came in 1962, when Karl F. Rolvaag defeated the incumbent Republican Elmer L. Andersen by a mere ninety-one votes. Ballot recounts, needed to finally decide the election, took four months to tally. A race that was certainly not close was the 1964 presidential contest won by Lyndon B. Johnson and his running mate Hubert Humphrey. Vice-President Humphrey was the first Minnesotan to hold a nationally elected office.

The grim Vietnam War divided the state as well as the nation. In 1968, President Johnson decided not to run for reelection. Minnesota Senator Eugene McCarthy ran for the Democratic presidential nomination, promising to end the war. McCarthy's campaign captured the loyalty of thousands of antiwar activists across the country. Opposing McCarthy was his old DFL colleague Hubert Humphrey. Insiders claimed that Vice-President Humphrey was privately opposed to the Vietnam War, but he remained loyal to Johnson and in his public speeches supported the policies of the president. In a bitter convention, the Democrats nominated Hubert Humphrey to be their candidate for president, marking the first time a Minnesotan received such an honor from a major party. Humphrey lost a close race to Republican Richard Nixon.

In recent years, Minnesota politicians have remained powerful in the national scene. In 1969, President Nixon named Warren Burger, of St. Paul, chief justice of the United States Supreme Court. A year later, Nixon appointed Harry Blackmun, of Rochester, an associate Supreme Court justice.

In 1976, another Minnesotan rose to the national spotlight when Walter F. Mondale was elected vice-president on the Democratic ticket with Jimmy Carter. Mondale was born in the

In 1978, the Minnesota Supreme Court showed its concern for the environment when it banned a mining company from dumping taconite waste products into Duluth's Lake Superior waters (right).

southern Minnesota town of Ceylon and graduated from the University of Minnesota. While serving in the United States Senate, he had a liberal voting record, supporting such issues as civil rights and federal aid to education. In 1984, the Democratic party made Mondale its candidate for president. He was soundly defeated by Ronald Reagan, winning majorities in only Washington, D.C., and in his home state—Minnesota.

Minnesota, one of the country's loveliest states, has long been a leader in conservation efforts. Environmentalists hailed the founding of Voyageurs National Park, near International Falls, in 1970. But the state faced a dire pollution problem from taconite, once thought of as the salvation of the mining industry. In the course of processing taconite, the Reserve Mining Company of Silver Bay routinely dumped tons of taconite waste material, called tailings, into the crystal-clear waters of Lake Superior. Scientists linked the tailings to cancer. Alarm turned to outrage when traces of tailings turned up in Duluth's drinking water. Reserve Mining Company was taken to court. After much complicated litigation, the Minnesota Supreme Court ordered the company to stop discharging tailings into Lake Superior. The court's decision was applauded as a major triumph for the environmentalists. In 1980, the company set up an on-land-waste-disposal site.

The first half of the 1980s saw economic setbacks on the state's farms and in the iron-range country. Farmers, encouraged by years of rising crop prices, went into debt to expand their operations. Crop prices dropped dramatically in the early 1980s, and farmers were unable to pay off their loans to the banks. Hundreds of small farms were taken over by banks and auctioned off to the highest bidder. The mining industry became depressed because foreign competition cut the demand for Minnesota iron ore. The work force in the mines dropped from fifteen thousand in 1979 to two thousand in 1986. Unemployment in some northern Minnesota mining towns reached 90 percent.

The state's most bitter labor strike since the Great Depression rocked Austin in 1985 and 1986. Meat packers at the Hormel Company walked off their jobs when the company cut their wages an average of two dollars an hour. Officials claimed that the cuts were needed to keep Hormel's products competitive, but union leaders pointed out that the corporation had enjoyed record profits the year before. The walkout divided Austin into hostile camps of strikers and nonstrikers. Governor Rudy Perpich was forced to call in the state militia to keep order.

Minnesota's economic picture brightened in the late 1980s. "High-tech" industries that produce electronic equipment and computers expanded in the Twin Cities area. Construction projects in downtown Minneapolis employed hundreds of workers. Even the mining industry rebounded as a cheaper dollar made it easier to sell Great Lakes iron ore overseas. In 1989, the mining work force climbed to six thousand. Referring to the iron-range country, a state official said, "There's a feeling of hope that a corner has been turned. You don't see the despair we once had."

Chapter 7

GOVERNMENT AND THE ECONOMY

GOVERNMENT AND THE ECONOMY

GOVERNMENT

Minnesota is governed according to rules laid down in its original constitution, adopted in 1858. More than one hundred amendments have been attached to the constitution over the years. Amendments to the constitution are approved by the voters during regular elections, or amendments may be brought up at a special constitutional convention.

The constitution divides the state government into three branches: the executive branch, which carries out laws; the legislative branch, which writes new laws and rescinds old ones; and the judicial branch, which interprets laws and hears court cases.

The executive branch is headed by the governor, who serves four years and can be reelected to any number of additional terms. The governor has wide powers of appointment, and names the heads of powerful state agencies and departments. The constitution also allows the governor to call special sessions of the legislature and to call out the state militia in times of emergency.

The legislative branch consists of a 67-member senate and a 134-member house of representatives. Senators serve four-year terms, while representatives hold office for two years. Legislators discuss proposed laws, called bills; when they approve a bill, it goes to the governor. The governor's signature makes the bill a law. The governor may veto (refuse to sign) a bill, but the legislative department can override the veto with a two-thirds majority vote in both the house of representatives and the senate.

The judicial branch consists of the court system. Minnesota's highest judicial body is the state supreme court, which is made up of a chief justice and eight associate justices. All supreme court justices are elected to six-year terms. The state's second-highest court is the court of appeals, made up of twelve judges elected for six-year terms. Minnesota has one district court with ten judicial districts, each with three or more judges. The court system hears criminal cases and settles squabbles among neighbors as well as lawsuits between giant corporations.

Financing the government is always a source of heated debate among political leaders. Minnesota's yearly budget runs more than $5 billion. Primary sources of revenue are a personal income tax, a sales tax, and a tax paid by mining companies based on the amount of minerals they take from the ground.

Local governments are administered by Minnesota's 87 counties, 855 cities, and nearly 1,800 townships. Providing for school systems and police forces are among the functions of local government.

EDUCATION

At a cost of almost $2.5 billion a year, the public school system is the largest single item in the state's budget. But Minnesotans are willing to pay to keep their schools among the best in the nation. Minnesota leads the country in the percentage of students who complete high school. Its high-school graduates consistently rank among those of the top five states in ACT college admission scores.

State law requires children to attend school from ages seven to sixteen. It costs taxpayers about $4,000 per year to educate each

Left: Students on the Mall at the University of Minnesota in Minneapolis
Above: The University of Minnesota Landscape Arboretum in Chanhassen

student. Minnesota teachers are among the highest paid in the nation. Statewide, about half a million elementary students and a quarter million secondary students start classes each fall.

Minnesota has twenty-seven degree-granting colleges and universities. The largest is the state-supported University of Minnesota, with its main campus in the Twin Cities. Other University of Minnesota campuses are located in Crookston, Duluth, Morris, and Waseca. The state's oldest private university is Hamline, which was founded in St. Paul in 1854. Augsburg College, in Minneapolis; Carleton College, in Northfield; the College of St. Catherine, in St. Paul; and St. John's University, in Collegeville, are among the state's privately supported colleges.

AGRICULTURE

Turning out $6 billion worth of farm products each year, Minnesota is among the top ten agricultural states. The Gopher State has about 96,000 farms, averaging 320 acres (130 hectares) in size.

Beef cattle (left) and peas (right) are among Minnesota's agricultural products.

Minnesota ranks first in the nation in the production of sugar beets, second in hay, third in oats, and fourth in soybeans, barley, and corn. The Red River Valley, which separates Minnesota and North Dakota, produces 17 million pounds (7.7 million kilograms) of potatoes a year. Minnesota's most valuable crops are corn, soybeans, and wheat. Apples, raspberries, strawberries, green peas, cabbages, carrots, dry beans, and onions are among the other crops grown in the state.

Minnesota is second only to Wisconsin in the production of dairy products. In fact, milk is the state's most valuable farm product. Poultry farms are numerous. Minnesota is America's second-largest turkey grower and a leading producer of eggs. Beef cattle, hogs, sheep, lambs, and broiler chickens are important sources of Minnesota's farm income.

MANUFACTURING

About 370,000 Minnesotans hold manufacturing jobs. Factories operating within the state produce more than $15 billion worth of manufactured goods each year. Nonelectrical machinery, food and food processing, and printing and publishing are the state's three major manufacturing industries. The computer business alone employs more than 81,000 Minnesotans.

Food-processing companies work in close cooperation with the state's farmers. Most of Minnesota's milk is processed into butter and cheese. Large meat-packing plants stand at Albert Lea, Austin, and Duluth. Flour mills, Minneapolis's first large industry, still operate in the Twin Cities. Companies connected to the mills turn out cereals and cake mixes. Sugar-beet refineries operate in the Red River Valley; soybean-oil plants, in and around the Twin Cities; and vegetable canning plants, in southern Minnesota. Nearly 46,000 Minnesotans are employed in the food-processing industry.

Other Minnesota manufacturing plants produce metal parts, paper products, scientific instruments, electrical machinery, and plastic goods.

NATURAL RESOURCES

Minnesota mines provide 70 percent of the nation's iron ore. Most of the ore taken from the soil is taconite. One geologist's report claimed that the Gopher State has enough taconite to last two hundred years at the present rate of output. Granite, limestone, clay, sand, and gravel are all quarried in Minnesota.

Minnesota's extensive forests provide wood for the pulp and paper industry. Today forestry is a carefully controlled enterprise, and loggers plant more trees than they chop down.

Commercial fishing is a $4-million-a-year industry in the state. Herring, smelt, whitefish, and lake trout are taken from Lake Superior; walleye from smaller lakes.

Tourist attractions, such as Historic Fort Snelling (left) and the St. Paul Winter Carnival (above), contribute to the state's economy.

SERVICES

The service industries are Minnesota's largest single employer. Service businesses do not produce a product, but rather provide customers with a service, such as a hotel room. Nearly half a million Minnesotans work in service-related businesses.

Tourism is the key to Minnesota's healthy service industry. Because of its incredible natural beauty and its wealth of recreational facilities, Minnesota earns about $5 billion a year through tourism. The state tourist office estimates that tourist dollars provide 110,000 jobs for Minnesotans.

Wholesale and retail trade is the most valuable service industry in the state. Although trade is carried on throughout the state, Duluth and the Twin Cities are the most important trade centers.

TRANSPORTATION AND COMMUNICATION

About 131,000 miles (210,818 kilometers) of roadways crisscross the Gopher State. Railroad passenger service has declined, but

Duluth is the nation's busiest freshwater port.

twelve major rail lines still haul thousands of tons of freight over
8,000 miles (12,874 kilometers) of track. One transportation
institution known by all American travelers is the Greyhound
Corporation, founded in Hibbing in 1914. Minnesota has about
420 airports. The largest is St. Paul-Minneapolis International
Airport, which is served by eight major airlines.

Water transportation remains vital to the state's economy. River
barges carry coal and oil up the Mississippi River to factories in
the Twin Cities, and grain and other Minnesota products
downriver. Duluth remains the busiest freshwater port in the
nation.

Minnesota has 30 daily newspapers and about 290 weeklies. The
largest daily newspapers are the *Star Tribune,* the *St. Paul Pioneer
Press Dispatch,* and the *Rochester Post-Bulletin.* The *St. Paul Pioneer
Press Dispatch* is descended from the *Minnesota Pioneer,* the state's
first newspaper, which began printing on a hand press in 1849.
Major magazines published in the state include *Family Handyman*
and *Catholic Digest.* Minnesota has about 190 radio stations and 18
television stations, including several television channels devoted
to education.

Chapter 8
ARTS AND LEISURE

ARTS AND LEISURE

Sports, fairs, literature, and the arts are a passion in the Gopher State. The people's devotion to culture began long before the state's founding.

THE FINE ARTS

Indian pictographs and rock paintings are the earliest examples of Minnesota art. The Indians reduced red ochre, an impure iron ore, to ash and mixed it with animal fat. They used this mixture to paint pictures of men, animals, and symbols on cliffs over lakes in the present-day Superior National Forest. Long-ago sculptors used the red rock quarried in Pipestone County to fashion intricately carved smoking pipes. Some of the pipes are now displayed in museums.

One of the earliest white artists in the region was the remarkable George Catlin. Originally a New York lawyer, Catlin journeyed west as a young man searching for "some branch or enterprise of the arts, on which to devote my whole lifetime." Catlin visited the Dakota of Minnesota in the 1830s and painted scenes of their villages and of the people going about everyday tasks.

Even the hardworking pioneers found time to admire the work of local artists. Danish immigrant Peter Clausen arrived in

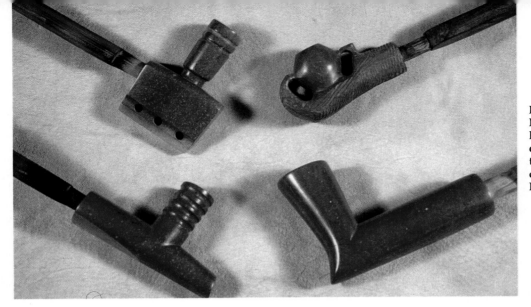

For centuries, Minnesota's Indians have carved beautiful objects, such as these pipes, from the catlinite found in Pipestone County.

Minnesota in the 1860s and did portraits of farmers and murals for church walls. Frontier artist Edwin Whitefield rendered watercolors of farms and forests. Homer D. Martin, a landscape artist from New York, came to St. Paul near the end of the pioneer period and enriched the state's art community.

The Minneapolis Society of Fine Arts, founded in 1883, eventually opened its own art school and gallery. In 1911, the Minneapolis Institute of Arts evolved from this society.

One artist who received her training at the society was Wanda Gág, who grew up in New Ulm and became a successful artist, writer, and illustrator in the early 1900s. One of Gág's most popular children's books was *Millions of Cats*, a work enlivened with comical illustrations.

Minnesota has been the home of several important sculptors. Norwegian-born sculptor Jacob Fjeld settled in Minnesota in the 1880s. Fjeld's best-known work is the sculpture *Hiawatha and Minnehaha*, which stands above Minnehaha Falls today. The artist's son, Paul Fjeld, was also a superb sculptor. Sculptor John Rood is known for many works, including a stylized gate he created for St. Paul's Hamline University. James Earle Fraser, who was born in Winona, designed the Indian head for the buffalo

Left: Jacob Fjeld's *Hiawatha and Minnehaha*, in Minnehaha Park
Above: The Minnesota Symphony Orchestra performing at Nicollet Mall

nickel and sculpted several statues for public buildings in
Washington, D.C.

The state's most renowned contemporary sculptor is Iranian-
born Siah Aramajani, who designed a striking pedestrian bridge
that leads to Minneapolis's Walker Art Center. Artist T. L. Solien,
of Pelican Rapids, renders abstract paintings sometimes inspired
by childhood memories. Another well-known abstract painter is
Steven Sorman, who lives in Marine-on-St. Croix.

MUSIC

Historically, music was of great importance to the Ojibwa
people. The Ojibwa had songs to mourn the dead, celebrate a
victory in war, bring rain, heal the sick, or make the corn grow
tall. The rattle and the drum were the primary instruments of the
Ojibwa. They used the flute only for love songs.

Thanks to musical historian Frances Densmore, songs of the Ojibwa, Dakota, and other Native American groups can still be heard and studied. Born in Red Wing in 1867, Densmore often heard compelling tribal songs chanted from a Dakota village across the river from her home. Densmore studied classical music, but the surging rhythms of the Native Americans remained etched in her thoughts. When the first phonographs became available, she carried the strange instrument to the reservations and made wax records of the music. These records, now in the Smithsonian Institution in Washington, D.C., serve as a vital link to the American past.

The Minnesota Symphony Orchestra was founded in 1903, largely through the efforts of Emil Oberhoffer, a composer, conductor, violinist, and tireless organizer. In the 1930s, the orchestra was directed by Eugene Ormandy, who became the world-renowned conductor of the Philadelphia Symphony Orchestra. One historian hailed the Minnesota Symphony as "Minnesota's outstanding contribution to the world of music."

In the 1960s, one of the great names in popular music was Bob Dylan. Born in Duluth and raised in the iron-range town of Hibbing, Dylan became a guitarist, singer, and composer. His songs of protest, such as "The Times They Are A-Changin' " and "Blowin' in the Wind," made Dylan the most influential folksinger of his time.

Today, Minnesota offers music for everyone's taste. Folk music is sung at the University of Minnesota's Twin Cities campus. The Minnesota Symphony Orchestra plays classical music at Orchestra Hall in Minneapolis, and the St. Paul Chamber Orchestra performs at the Ordway Music Theater in St. Paul. Dozens of small towns also have orchestras. The Minnesota Opera Company, based in St. Paul, specializes in English-language works. The

The Minnesota Opera Company performs at the Ordway Music Theater in St. Paul.

St. Olaf College Choir at Northfield is a nationally known vocal group that sings *a cappella* (without accompaniment).

THEATER

Minnesotans show a phenomenal interest in theater. The Twin Cities area, known as one of the nation's most exciting and fertile theater centers, hosts some ninety different theaters and playhouses. Many of these theaters are found in a renovated warehouse district near downtown Minneapolis. The Tyrone Guthrie Theater, founded by Sir Tyrone Guthrie in Minneapolis in 1963, houses one of America's finest repertory theater groups.

Other important theaters in Minneapolis include the internationally famed Children's Theatre Company; the Mixed

Blood Theater, which presents bold, new works; and Theatre in the Round, the city's oldest community theater. The Actors Theatre of St. Paul performs contemporary and classical plays. The Theatre de la Jeune Lune, whose company spends half the year in France, produces plays presented in English but styled in the European tradition.

LITERATURE

Political thought during the frontier era was influenced by Jane Grey Swisshelm, a crusading newspaper owner who moved to St. Cloud in 1857. The first woman in the nation to write a political news column, Swisshelm became one of America's most talked-about women. In her editorials, she championed two main causes: rights for women and the abolition of slavery. Her fearless editorial stance created bitter enemies. Many hotel owners feared that they would lose the business of southern slaveholders who came north for the summer. But even after receiving death threats and having her newspaper office vandalized, Swisshelm continued to express her views.

Writing as well as frontier politics was the domain of multitalented Ignatius Donnelly. In addition to holding political offices, he wrote novels such as *Caesar's Column*, which predicted the coming of a terrible war in which aircraft would be used to drop bombs. His nonfiction books included *The Great Cryptogram*, in which he argued that the works of William Shakespeare were actually written by Francis Bacon. Although critics generally gave his books poor reviews, he enjoyed fantastic success with the reading public. Donnelly's *Atlantis*, a nonfiction book about the fabled lost continent, was reprinted in fifty editions and translated into many languages.

Minnesota writers Thorstein Veblen, Ole Rolvaag, and Charles M. Flandreau enjoyed wide audiences in the early twentieth century. Veblen graduated from Carleton College in Northfield and became an economist and social critic. His *Theory of the Leisure Class* criticized the life-styles and spending habits of rich Americans. Ole Rolvaag, a Norwegian immigrant, was a professor at St. Olaf College in Northfield. His stunning novel *Giants in the Earth* was hailed by one critic as "the most powerful novel that has ever been written about pioneer life in America." Charles Flandreau was a gifted journalist and travel writer who was born in St. Paul. His *Viva Mexico* is a fascinating account of that country in the early 1900s.

One of the great writers of the 1920s was Sinclair Lewis, born in Sauk Centre in 1885. In such books as *Main Street, Babbitt,* and *Elmer Gantry,* he attacked what he perceived as weaknesses in American society. In 1930, Sinclair Lewis won the Nobel Prize for literature, becoming the first American to be presented with that honor.

Novelist and short-story writer F. Scott Fitzgerald is associated with high society in New York and Paris, but had his roots in Minnesota. Born in St. Paul, Fitzgerald lived for many years on Summit Avenue in the Minnesota capital. A leading writer of the 1920s, Fitzgerald wrote books that explore the pleasure-seeking but morally empty lives of the upper class. *The Great Gatsby,* about a fabulously rich but unhappy man, is an American classic.

World War II and the postwar era produced many outstanding Minnesota writers. Max Shulman, a University of Minnesota graduate, delighted readers with his comic novel *Barefoot Boy with Cheek.* Thomas Heggin, of Minneapolis, wrote the bittersweet World War II book *Mr. Roberts,* which became a long-running play and a popular movie. Minnesota resident Carol R. Brink was

Writers Sinclair Lewis (left) and F. Scott Fitzgerald (right) and musician
Bob Dylan (middle) are among the artists who have hailed from Minnesota.

a gifted writer of children's books, including the charming novel
Caddie Woodlawn, about a pioneer girl.

Robert Bly, born in Madison and now a resident of Moose Lake,
is one of the nation's most influential modern poets. Bly won the
National Book Award in poetry and received grants from the
Guggenheim Foundation. In addition to original writing, Bly
translates poems from Swedish, German, and Spanish. One of his
collections of poems is called *Silence in the Snowy Fields*.

In recent years, several Minnesota humorists have captured
national attention, including Howard Mohr, who wrote the
rollicking best-seller *How to Talk Minnesotan*. Even more famous is
humorist Garrison Keillor. In the 1970s and 1980s, Keillor hosted
''A Prairie Home Companion,'' a national radio variety program
broadcast from St. Paul. During the show, Keillor told stories—in
a deadpan but strangely compelling voice—about the hilarious

antics of people in a fictional Minnesota town called Lake Wobegon. Lake Wobegon, he said, was a place where "the women are strong, the men good-looking, and the children all above average." Keillor's books *Lake Wobegon Days* and *Leaving Home* both became best-sellers.

SPORTS

Minnesota is a sports-crazy state. Softball, high-school basketball, soccer, and a dozen other team sports are followed with great enthusiasm. There are 2,255 registered amateur hockey teams in Minnesota — more than in any other state. The University of Minnesota has fielded many powerhouse football, basketball, and hockey teams.

The Minnesota Vikings have a proud history in the National Football League. Over the years, their offensive squads have featured such sharp quarterbacks as Fran Tarkenton and Wade Wilson, and such lightning-quick wide receivers as Ahmad Rashad and Anthony Carter. In the 1970s, the Vikings were feared throughout their league for a hard-hitting defensive line that was nicknamed "the Purple People Eaters" after the color of their uniforms. The powerful Vikings appeared in four Super Bowl games of the 1970s.

Baseball's Minnesota Twins are another team with a winning tradition. In the 1960s and 1970s, the Twins were led by the mighty slugger Harmon Killebrew, the fifth-leading home-run hitter in baseball history. Teaming with Killebrew was Rod Carew, perhaps the best pure hitter of the modern era. In 1987, when the Twins thrilled the state by winning the World Series, they were led by pitcher Frank Viola and outfielder Kirby Puckett.

In professional hockey, the Minnesota North Stars of the

Above: The United States Hockey Hall of Fame in Eveleth
Right: The Minnesota Twins during a game at the Metrodome

National Hockey League enjoy great popularity. Minneapolis once hosted a professional basketball team called the Lakers, but the team moved to Los Angeles in 1960. Professional basketball revisited Minnesota in 1989, when the Timberwolves opened as an expansion team of the National Basketball Association.

FAIRS AND FUN

It is safe to say that on any weekend of the year, some Minnesota community is hosting a fair. There are fairs to celebrate the state's past, to honor the ethnic diversity of its people, or just to have a bit of fun. The Minnesota State Fair is the largest annual party hosted by the state. Held in St. Paul in late August, it attracts more than one million people each year.

Ethnic festivals offer food, music and dance, and arts and crafts. The Indian Culture Festival, held every August at Mille Lacs,

The displays at Minnesota's hundreds of festivals range from the Indian crafts at the Big Island Rendezvous at Helmer Myre State Park (left) to the ice sculptures at St. Paul's Winter Carnival (above).

celebrates the Ojibwas' ancient devotion to music. Svenskarnas Dag (Swedish Day) is marked by brass bands, a Swedish choir, and folk dances held at Minnehaha Park in Minneapolis each June. Tyler's Danish community celebrates Aebleskiver Day, which features a grand parade down the main street and street dancing at night. Finnish food and music are featured at the Sisu Finnish Festival at Embarrass. The town of Faribault hosts Czech Heritage Days, during which guests are invited to feast on delicious Czech food.

Minnesota's proud past is relived in many festivals. New Ulm hosts the Blacksmith and Frontier Life Pageant, which features lectures on pioneer life and blacksmithing demonstrations. An ancient gristmill is operated during Grinding Days at Argyle. The town of Cloquet relives a rough-and-tumble time in Minnesota history during Lumberjack Days.

Minnesota's voyageur era is celebrated during the Snake River Rendezvous, held every September in Pine City.

A wildly popular St. Paul event is the Winter Carnival, held in January. The carnival was first held, more than a century ago, after a New York City newspaper writer complained that a St. Paul winter was unfit even for polar bears. Ice-skating races, ski-jumping and ice-sculpting contests, and a parade are all part of the festival. In 1986, the one-hundredth anniversary of the carnival, St. Paul built the world's tallest ice palace.

Of course, many Minnesota festivals are given simply as an excuse for people to gather and have a good time. During Verga Loony Days, people dress in outrageous costumes and march in a "Loony Parade." Nerstrand Bologna Days feature a bologna-eating contest. The Pelican Rapids Ugly Truck Contest awards a prize to the most beat-up, rusted-out pickup truck in the county.

Chapter 9

A TOUR OF THE GOPHER STATE

A TOUR OF THE GOPHER STATE

Minnesota has sixty-four state parks, Voyageurs National Park, two national forests, nearly 10,000 miles (16,093 kilometers) of hiking trails, and endless canoe streams. Its cities hold fascinating museums as well as architectural surprises. It would be impossible to experience all that the Gopher State has to offer, but even a brief tour can fill a traveler with enough memories to last a lifetime.

SOUTHERN MINNESOTA

Some of the state's oldest towns are found along the Mississippi River south of the Twin Cities. La Crescent was a logging boomtown in the 1850s. Today, La Crescent is surrounded by apple orchards and is called the Apple Capital of Minnesota. Winona is highlighted by 500-foot (152-meter) limestone bluffs that rise majestically from its riverbanks. It is believed that the town's name came from a despairing Dakota girl named Wi-No-Nah who leaped off one of the bluffs rather than marry someone whom she did not love. To the north is Lake City, gateway to lovely Lake Pepin. Townspeople claim that the sport of waterskiing was invented on Lake Pepin in 1922, when a local daredevil tried to balance on skis while tied to the back of a speeding motorboat. Farther north along the Mississippi is Red Wing, once a major pottery producer. Elegant stoneware is still sold in Red Wing's historic district.

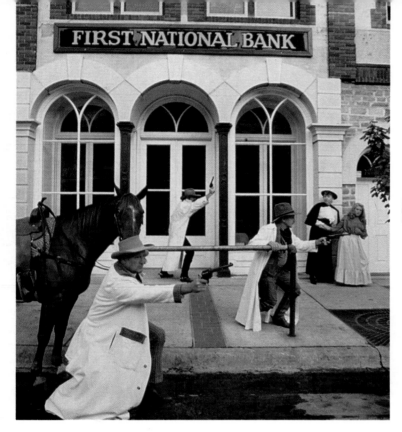

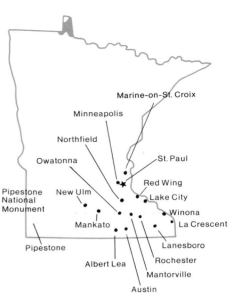

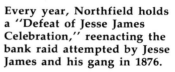

Every year, Northfield holds a "Defeat of Jesse James Celebration," reenacting the bank raid attempted by Jesse James and his gang in 1876.

Driving west from the Mississippi River, a traveler in southern Minnesota encounters lush woods. Anglers say the best trout fishing in the state is found at Whitewater State Park near Altura. Watercress grows in spring-fed ponds at Beaver Creek Valley State Park, near Caledonia. Architectural gems stand out among the delightful old houses in Lanesboro and in Mantorville.

East of Mantorville is Rochester, home of the Mayo Clinic and Minnesota's fifth-largest city. Its most prominent house is a thirty-eight-room mansion called Mayowood, which once belonged to the Mayo family. Open to the public, Mayowood is crammed with antiques and artworks. Northwest of Rochester is Northfield, a quiet college town that has an interesting past. On September 7, 1876, outlaw Jesse James and his gang shot up Northfield in a bloody attempt to rob the town's largest bank. The people of Northfield foiled the robbery and killed two gang members. Every

Above: New Ulm's glockenspiel
Right: A building in Pipestone
constructed of catlinite

year, on the weekend after Labor Day, the robbery is reenacted.

Directly south, history also comes alive in Owatonna's Village of Yesteryear, a complex of nine restored pioneer buildings that date to the mid-1800s. Farther south lies Austin, where scientists at the Hormel Institute, a graduate school of the University of Minnesota, study the effect of diet on health.

The town of Albert Lea, west of Austin, is an agricultural center named after the army officer who surveyed the region in 1835. More than four hundred species of wildflowers greet visitors at the nearby Helmer Myre State Park. To the northwest, the city of Mankato lies in a forested valley where the Blue Earth and Minnesota rivers meet. Relics of Mankato's pioneer past are displayed at the Blue Earth County Historical Society. Between Mankato and the town of Judson sprawls Minneopa State Park, which holds two surging waterfalls.

During the great Dakota War of 1862, the streets of New Ulm

were the scene of ferocious hand-to-hand fighting between settlers and Indian warriors. Defender's Monument, near the courthouse, commemorates those who died during the conflict. Also in New Ulm is a fantastic glockenspiel, a 45-foot- (14-meter-) tall musical clock tower complete with moving figures.

The Minnesota River Valley forms the heart of Fort Ridgely State Park, which lies near Fairfax. More than 10 miles (16 kilometers) of hiking trails wind along the park's wooded ravines. Sibley State Park, near the town of Willmar, is also a hiker's delight, with trails leading beside scenic overlooks, lakes, and farmland.

The southwest corner of Minnesota is sometimes called Pipestone Country, after a rock quarry that the ancient Indians of the area believed was sacred. It is primarily flat land that once supported a vast tall-grass prairie roamed by buffalo. At Blue Mounds State Park near Luverne rises a massive quartzite cliff over which Dakota hunters drove buffalo herds to their death.

The city of Pipestone is graced with many turn-of-the-century buildings. The Pipestone County Museum, built in 1896, is a handsome example of red stone construction. Just north of the city is the Pipestone National Monument, the site of the ancient quarry. A Dakota legend holds that the two-thousand-year-old tribe originated from this spot, and that the stone has a reddish color because it is drenched with the blood of Dakota ancestors.

METROLAND

The Gopher State's Metroland begins at the St. Croix River and spreads west to envelop the Twin Cities and their suburbs. Although Metroland is the state's most populous region, it also contains quaint towns and wilderness attractions. Afton State

The Twin Cities of St. Paul (left) and Minneapolis (right) form one of the most livable big-city complexes in the United States.

Park, near Hastings, features 1,700 acres (688 hectares) of forested hills. To the north is the village of Marine-on-St. Croix, whose lovely old houses make it an artists' retreat.

South of the Twin Cities lies Fort Snelling, the historic soul of Minnesota. Completed in the 1820s, the fort remained an active army post until 1946. Today, the fort's grounds are open to the public. Visitors may tour the seventeen restored buildings that still stand. "Soldiers" dressed in 1820s army uniforms engage in rifle practice and cannon firing.

All Minnesotans know that Minneapolis and St. Paul are more like fraternal twins than identical twins. St. Paul tends to be conservative and perhaps a bit more reserved, while Minneapolis is more progressive and modern. Taken together, however, they form one of the most livable big-city complexes in the United States. The Twin Cities are clean, have a low crime rate, and are packed with excitement.

The marvelous State Capitol rises in the center of St. Paul. Completed in 1905, it has one of the largest self-supporting marble domes in the world. Twenty-two different types of marble went into its construction. The State Capitol was designed by St. Paul resident Cass Gilbert, the same architect who designed the Supreme Court building in Washington, D.C.

Museums abound in Minnesota's capital city. Next to the State Capitol is the Minnesota Historical Society, where exhibits dramatize state history. Guests at Technology Hall of the Minnesota Science Museum operate mechanical arms and talk to computers. The Minnesota Museum of Art holds masterpieces of American as well as Asian art. Children play with mind-boggling puzzles and enjoy other "hands-on" exhibits at St. Paul's Children's Museum.

St. Paul residents can relax in more than 2,000 acres (809 hectares) of parkland. Six mounds, built in the distant past, are the highlight of Indian Mounds Park. Waterfalls and artificial streams flow in Town Square Park, said to be the nation's largest indoor park. Como Park boasts a zoo and a conservatory. Rice Park is the city's oldest and perhaps most beloved park. In January, fabulous ice sculptures—the hit of the city's winter carnival—stand in Rice Park.

The capital city is a living display of architecture. The fifteen-room Alexander Ramsey House has historic as well as architectural appeal. Another architectural landmark is the St. Paul Hotel, built in 1910 and completely refurbished in the 1970s. Superb Victorian mansions, including James J. Hill's home, line St. Paul's Summit Avenue. At the end of Summit stands the

St. Paul's many parks include historic Rice Park (left) and lush Como Park (right).

grandiose St. Paul Cathedral, one of America's finest examples of church architecture.

Minneapolis, the Gopher State's biggest and busiest city, lies across the Mississippi River from St. Paul. From the city's historic Falls of St. Anthony spreads the gleaming downtown area, with its well-known landmarks, such as the fifty-seven-story IDS Tower and the lively pedestrian mall at Nicollet Avenue. The enclosed pedestrian bridges, or skyways, that connect some of Minneapolis's downtown buildings are individually designed and strikingly different from one another. The skyway system protects people moving among the downtown buildings from the chill of winter and the heat of summer. Street life is almost constant in downtown Minneapolis, as people stroll to the many theaters or hustle to the Hubert H. Humphrey Metrodome, where the Twins and the Vikings play.

Minneapolis boasts twenty-two lakes, all surrounded by parkland. The city has 153 parks and 45 miles (72 kilometers) of

Left: City Center, a shopping complex in downtown Minneapolis
Right: The monorail that runs above the Minnesota Zoo's animal habitats

bicycle and jogging paths. One of Minneapolis's most popular retreats is Minnehaha Park, where Minnehaha Falls tumbles over a ravine. Near downtown is Loring Park, which harbors a lake and a bird sanctuary. The Walker Art Center, Guthrie Theater, and Minnesota Sculpture Garden are nearby.

Museum lovers find many exciting exhibits in Minneapolis. On the University of Minnesota campus is the James Ford Bell Museum of Natural History, which exhibits Minnesota wildlife. More than two thousand stars light up the indoor skies at the Minneapolis Planetarium, housed in the public library. The state's Scandinavian heritage is honored at Minneapolis's American Swedish Institute. The classic Minneapolis Institute of Arts and the contemporary Walker Art Center are internationally recognized art museums.

Certainly a highlight of Metroland is the Minnesota Zoo, located in suburban Apple Valley. Spreading over 480 acres (194 hectares), the zoo contains 1,700 animals. Wildlife experts

The boyhood home of aviator Charles Lindbergh is preserved at Charles A. Lindbergh State Park in Little Falls.

rank it as one of America's top ten zoos. A spectacular overview of the zoo is gained by riding the unique Sky Trail, a monorail train that runs above the animals' settings.

CENTRAL MINNESOTA

One of the state's many exciting scenic drives winds north along the St. Croix River past three central Minnesota state parks. The William O'Brien State Park offers year-round entertainment with hiking trails and cross-country ski routes. Interstate State Park at Taylors Falls features towering cliffs and sandstone bluffs. Miles of woodland trails and rushing streams greet visitors farther north at Wild River State Park.

The Great Hinckley Fire of 1894 leveled the town and the surrounding forest. The tragedy is recalled at the city's Hinckley Fire Museum. A 32-mile (51-kilometer) woodland trail—which serves snowmobiles in the winter and bicycles in the summer—leads from Hinckley to Moose Lake.

To the west is Mille Lacs Lake. Anglers call this lake a "walleye factory" because of the tremendous number of fighting game fish pulled out of its waters. At the lakeshore town of Garrison stands a statue of a giant walleye. In the dead of winter, five thousand or more hardy ice fishermen cover frozen Mille Lacs Lake, all hoping to hook a big one.

To the southwest lies Little Falls, the boyhood home of aviator Charles Lindbergh. The house in which Lindbergh grew up has been restored to look as it did at the turn of the century. Directly to the south is St. Cloud, central Minnesota's biggest city. A fine park system and miles of bicycle paths are highlights of St. Cloud. Neighboring Richmond lies in the middle of the Horseshoe Chain of Lakes.

Nobel Prizewinning author Sinclair Lewis was Sauk Centre's most famous resident. It is commonly believed that Sauk Centre was the model for the fictional town of Gopher Prairie in Lewis's novel *Main Street*.

Farther west, Alexandria claims to be the "Birthplace of America" because the Kensington Runestone, dated 1362, was discovered nearby. The controversial stone is displayed today at the city's Runestone Museum. Housed in the Grant County Historical Museum at Elbow Lake is a collection of oxcarts used by the pioneers.

A bit to the south, the spectacular Glacier Ridge Trail lures hikers and bicyclists to Glacier Lakes State Park near Starbuck. Big Stone Lake State Park, which lies along the Red River near Ortonville, attracts swimmers as well as hikers.

THE NORTHWEST

More than twelve hundred lakes dot the sprawling Chippewa National Forest, which covers more than 2 million acres

(0.8 million hectares) of northwestern Minnesota. Largest of the lakes are Leech Lake and Lake Winnibigoshish—or Big Winnie, as the locals call it. Northwestern Minnesota is one of many regions that claim close ties to the mythical lumberjack Paul Bunyan, one of American folklore's most beloved characters. Legend has it that the region's many lakes were formed by the colossal footprints of Bunyan's giant blue pet ox, Babe.

Bicycle and horseback riders enjoy the Heartland State Trail, which runs from Park Rapids to Walker with stops at Akeley and Nevis. Akeley, which, like several Minnesota towns, claims to be the birthplace of Paul Bunyan, has a gigantic statue of baby Paul in his cradle. Paul Bunyan lore continues at the town of Bemidji, which boasts a huge statue of the lumberjack and the ox.

The Mississippi River begins its 2,500-mile (4,023-kilometer) journey to the Gulf of Mexico at lovely Lake Itasca. Visitors take the famed "fifteen steps" across an ankle-deep creek that later becomes the broad river the Indians called Father of Waters. Founded in 1891, Itasca State Park was Minnesota's first state park and remains one of its most popular. Hikers there explore Indian burial mounds within the park's 32,000 acres (12,950 hectares) of woodland. To the southwest is the city of Detroit Lakes. Its residents have a difficult time deciding where to fish; there are 412 lakes within a 25-mile (40-kilometer) radius of the town's center.

Situated along the Red River on the state's western border is Moorhead, home of Concordia College and Moorhead State University. In Moorhead is Comstock House, a one-hundred-year-old mansion that is now a museum displaying Red River regional history. To the north is Crookston, where the Polk County Historical Museum holds relics from America's British past. The village of Thief River Falls, to the northeast, provides the gateway

Giant statues of mythical lumberjack Paul Bunyan and his great blue ox, Babe, stand in Bemidji.

to the Agassiz National Wildlife Refuge, where deer, wolves, moose, and bears roam freely.

To the northeast is sprawling Lake of the Woods, which Minnesota shares with Canada. Jutting into the lake is the Northwest Angle, a peninsula that is the northernmost point of the lower forty-eight states. The Northwest Angle can be reached only by driving through Canada or by taking a boat across Lake of the Woods. Because of a surveyor's error in the 1820s, the Northwest Angle is separated from the United States' land boundaries.

THE NORTHEAST

In northeastern Minnesota is iron-range country. Visitors may take the Iron Trail, Highway 169, through Coleraine, Calumet, Taconite, Keewatin, Hibbing, Chisholm, Mountain Iron, Virginia,

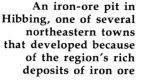

An iron-ore pit in Hibbing, one of several northeastern towns that developed because of the region's rich deposits of iron ore

and other iron-range towns that grew because of the region's rich deposits of iron ore. Hibbing offers a tour of the Hull-Rust Mine, the world's largest open-pit iron-ore mine. The Iron Man Memorial, a 36-foot (11-meter) brass and copper sculpture, greets visitors at Chisholm. Ironworld USA, a park near Chisholm, celebrates the contributions of the many ethnic groups that came to the range country seeking mining jobs.

Hockey buffs flock to the northeastern Minnesota town of Eveleth, home of the U.S. Hockey Hall of Fame. Amateur hockey is celebrated at the museum, and the gold-medal-winning U.S. Olympic teams of 1960 and 1980 are especially honored. At nearby Biwabik is the Giants Ridge Ski Area, which offers skiers fifteen challenging downhill runs and miles of cross-country routes.

Far to the north, hugging the Canadian border, is International Falls. Converting trees into paper and pulp is big business in International Falls, and several mills offer tours of the process. Rainy River and Rainy Lake serve as the city's playgrounds.

Historians at the nearby Grand Mound Interpretive Center give lectures and slide shows on the mound-building Indians who lived along the Rainy River some two thousand years ago.

A stellar attraction of northeast Minnesota is Voyageurs National Park. Dedicated to the French-Canadian voyageurs who once journeyed here, the park contains 218,000 acres (88,222 hectares) of wilderness wonders. Visitors find endless streams and thirty major lakes in the park. The best way to view its secrets is aboard a boat. The winding rivers provide exciting avenues for canoeists. During the summer months, naturalists take groups on hikes and discovery trips.

THE ARROWHEAD COUNTRY

Lush and unspoiled forests cover most of the Arrowhead region, but its gateway is found at Duluth—the state's third-largest city. Despite the ups and downs of the iron-ore industry, Duluth remains a busy port. Its most distinctive landmark is the Aerial Lift Bridge—the largest such bridge in the world—that moves up and down to permit the passage of oceangoing ships. Visitors to the city are invited to tour the Canal Park Marine Museum, which tells the story of Great Lakes shipping. Offshore is the *William A. Irvin*, a retired Great Lakes ore carrier that is now a floating museum. The Duluth Zoological Gardens hold more than five hundred animals. A lively Duluth attraction is the St. Louis County Heritage and Arts Center. Popularly called the Depot, this restored 1890s train station contains several museums and theaters.

Northeast of Duluth, and hugging the Lake Superior shoreline, is a 150-mile (241-kilometer) strip of land known as the North Shore. Along this lakeside portion of the Arrowhead is

Duluth's Aerial Lift Bridge (left) and the Boundary Waters Canoe Area (right) are two well-known Arrowhead region landmarks.

Gooseberry Falls State Park near Two Harbors. The Gooseberry River tumbles 100 feet (30 meters) over two magnificent waterfalls into Lake Superior. Four wilderness lakes and miles of rugged hiking trails greet visitors at Tettegouche State Park north of Silver Bay. Silver Bay is the home of Reserve Mining Company, which offers tours of its large-scale taconite plants. The town of Grand Marais is a quiet fishing village that enjoys Lake Superior in its front yard, and Eagle Mountain—Minnesota's highest point—in its backyard.

Above the North Shore spreads the vast Superior National Forest. From Grand Marais, travelers may take the 63-mile (101-kilometer) Gunflint Trail, a road that leads into the depths of this national forest. Nestled in the forest's 3 million acres (1.2 million hectares) are more than two thousand lakes. Few highways penetrate this woodland, but canoeists paddle through its heart over the world-famed Boundary Waters Canoe Area. Lonely and lovely, the Superior National Forest holds far more

Breathtaking waterfalls are the hallmark of Gooseberry Falls State Park.

moose, deer, bears, and timber wolves than it does people. Its largest community is the iron-mining and resort town of Ely. During the frigid month of January, Ely hosts the world's best mushers at the annual All-American Sled Dog Championships.

At the tip of the Arrowhead Country lies the town of Grand Portage and Grand Portage National Monument. In the 1700s, the town served as a base camp for the North West Company's voyageurs. It is generally considered to be the first permanent European settlement in Minnesota. At Grand Portage National Monument, ranger-historians dressed in costumes from that period give talks on voyageur life.

The tip of the historic, rugged Arrowhead region ends the tour of the Gopher State. Modern, progressive Minnesota continues to thrive because of its hardworking people, diverse industries, and productive farms. Its cities are exciting places to visit, and its forests and lakes contain scenery so breathtaking that the state deserves to be called the Star of the North.

FACTS AT A GLANCE

GENERAL INFORMATION

Statehood: May 11, 1858, thirty-second state

Origin of Name: From a Dakota word meaning "sky-tinted water"

State Capital: St. Paul, since 1849

State Nicknames: Gopher State, North Star State, Land of 10,000 Lakes, Land of Sky-Blue Waters, and Bread and Butter State

State Flag: Minnesota's flag shows a version of the state seal on a blue background. On the seal are three dates: 1819 (the date of first white settlement), 1858 (statehood), and 1893 (the year the flag was adopted). The nineteen stars on the flag represent Minnesota's entry into the Union as the nineteenth state after the original thirteen.

State Motto: *L'Etoile du Nord*, French words meaning "The Star of the North"

State Bird: Common loon

State Flower: Showy lady's slipper

State Tree: Red (Norway) pine

State Grain: Wild rice

State Gemstone: Lake Superior agate

State Fish: Walleye

State Song: "Hail Minnesota," words by Truman E. Rickard and Arthur E. Upson; music by Truman E. Rickard:

> Minnesota hail to thee!
> Hail to thee, our state so dear!
> Thy light shall ever be
> A beacon bright and clear.
> Thy sons and daughters true
> Will proclaim thee near and far.
> They shall guard thy fame and adore thy name;
> Thou shalt be their northern star.

POPULATION

Population: 4,075,970, twenty-first among the states (1980 census)

Population Density: 48.3 persons per sq. mi. (18.6 persons per km^2)

Population Distribution: 67 percent of Minnesota's population live in cities or towns. About 70 percent of those urban Minnesotans live in the Twin Cities metropolitan area.

Minneapolis	370,951
St. Paul	270,230
Duluth	92,811
Bloomington	81,831
Rochester	57,906
Edina	46,073
Brooklyn Park	43,332
St. Louis Park	42,931
St. Cloud	42,566
Minnetonka	38,683

(Population figures according to 1980 census)

Population Growth: Minnesota has experienced steady and sometimes rapid growth over the years. In the years immediately following statehood, thousands flocked there to farm its fertile soils and work its rich mines. Since 1900, the population has grown more slowly. The state grew 7.1 percent from 1970 to 1980, a figure below the national average.

Year	Population
1850	6,077
1860	172,023
1870	439,706
1880	780,733
1890	1,310,283
1900	1,751,394
1920	2,387,125
1940	2,792,300
1950	2,982,483
1960	3,413,864
1970	3,806,103
1980	4,075,970

GEOGRAPHY

Borders: Minnesota is bordered by the Canadian provinces of Manitoba and Ontario to the north, Lake Superior and Wisconsin to the east, Iowa to the south, and North Dakota and South Dakota to the west.

The reconstructed North West Company trading post at Grand Portage National Monument

Highest Point: Eagle Mountain, in Cook County, 2,301 ft. (701 m)

Lowest Point: Along Lake Superior, 602 ft. (183 m)

Greatest Distances: North to south—411 mi. (661 km)
East to west—357 mi. (575 km)

Area: 84,402 sq. mi. (218,601 km²)

Rank in Area Among the States: Twelfth

National Forests and Parklands: Minnesota has two national monuments. Grand Portage National Monument, on the northwest shore of Lake Superior, marks the site of a historic canoe route and trading post. Pipestone National Monument, in the southwest part of the state, is the site of red stone deposits that were used for centuries by Indians to make peace pipes. Minnesota's only national park, Voyageurs National Park, near International Falls, contains many scenic waterways. The huge Superior National Forest, in the northeast corner of the state, includes the Boundary Waters Canoe Area. This is the nation's only wilderness area preserved for canoeists. Chippewa National Forest covers much of Itasca, Beltrami, and Cass counties, as well as the Leech Lake Indian Reservation.

Rivers: Waters from Minnesota flow north to Hudson Bay, east to the Atlantic Ocean, and south to the Gulf of Mexico. The most important of the state's rivers is the mighty Mississippi River. It has its source in Lake Itasca in the state's north-central region. The Mississippi and its tributaries, including the Crow Wing,

Dogsledding on Lake Phalen

Minnesota, Rum, St. Croix, and Sauk rivers, drain 57 percent of the state. Two major rivers, the Rainy River and Red River of the North, drain the northern and northwestern regions of the state. They flow north, toward Hudson Bay. The St. Louis River, which drains the area north of Lake Superior, flows into that great lake.

Lakes: There may be as many as twenty-two thousand lakes in Minnesota. These lakes cover 6 percent of Minnesota's area. Prehistoric glaciers that visited, and then retreated from, present-day Minnesota left thousands of shimmering blue gems of fresh water. They range in size from massive Lake Superior, the largest lake in the world at 31,700 sq. mi. (82,103 km²), to tiny ponds that provide water for a farmer's livestock. Lake of the Woods covers more than 2,000 sq. mi. (5,180 km²) in Minnesota and Canada. Red Lake, at 430 sq. mi. (1,114 km²), is the largest lake located entirely within Minnesota's borders. Other large lakes include Mille Lacs Lake, Leech Lake, and Lake Winnibigoshish.

Topography: Four main topographical regions extend over Minnesota. The Superior Upland, in the northeastern part of the state, is an extension of the Canadian Shield, composed of massive hard rock that withstood the glaciers. This area includes a region known as the Arrowhead Country. Minnesota's tallest point, Eagle Mountain, is located here. The Young Drift Plains, which spread over most of southern Minnesota and hug the western border, cover about half the state. This is a region of gently rolling farmland with soils deposited by glacial movement. The Dissected Till Plains, a small area in the southwest corner of the state, consist of lands covered with glacial till from the second-to-last glacier. The few level areas in the Dissected Till Plains provide excellent farming. The Driftless Area covers the southeast corner of the state. This zone, unaffected by the glaciers, contains swift-flowing streams that cut deep valleys.

Climate: Television weather reports during the winter often refer to International Falls, Minnesota, as the Nation's Icebox. January temperatures in this northern Minnesota border town average a high of only 14° F. (-10° C) and a low

Minnesota's varied flora includes birches (above) and such wildflowers as prairie phlox (right).

of -8° F. (-22° C). January temperatures in Minneapolis-St. Paul average a high of 23° F. (-5° C) and a low of 6° F. (-14° C). The lowest recorded temperature in Minnesota was -59° F. (-51° C), at Leech Lake Dam on February 9, 1899, and at Pokegama Falls on February 16, 1903.

Comfortable summer temperatures bring out the Minnesotans, as well as thousands of tourists, each year. The Minneapolis-St. Paul area has July highs of 85° F. (29° C) and lows of 63° F. (17° C). Even International Falls has balmy temperatures—July highs of 79° F. (26° C) and lows of 53° F. (12° C). But Minnesota, despite its northern location, can also get intensely hot in the summertime. Minnesota's record high temperature was a sweltering 114° F. (46° C), at Beardsley on July 29, 1927, and at Moorhead on July 6, 1936.

Precipitation varies from about 19 in. (48 cm) in the northwest to about 32 in. (81 cm) in the southeast. Snowfall also differs throughout the state. Southwest counties may see only 20 in. (51 cm) of annual snowfall, compared with 70 in. (178 cm) in the northeast. The growing season lasts about 160 days in south-central and southeastern Minnesota, while the north has a growing season of about 100 days.

NATURE

Trees: Jack pine, red pine, white pine, white birch, yellow birch, aspen, pin cherry, white spruce, balsam, fir, poplar, oak, mountain ash, red maple, wild plum, black spruce, tamarack, white cedar, hard maple, basswood, white elm, red elm, hickory, cottonwood, box elder

Wild Plants: Lotus (water lily), elder, sweet fern, thimbleberry, honeysuckle, blueberry, black and red raspberry, cranberry, snowberry, huckleberry, labrador tea, wintergreen, phlox, dwarf Ralmia, arbutus, showy lady's slipper, ironwood, dogwood, sumac, thorn apple, black haw, cattail, goldenrod, primrose, milkweed, morning glory, verbena, mint, bluebell, ragweed, thistle, anemone

Timber wolves (above) and moose (right) can still be found in Minnesota's northern wilderness areas.

Animals: Gopher, white-tailed deer, black bear, moose, elk, bobcat, timber wolf, lynx, red and grey squirrel, skunk, cottontail and snowshoe rabbit, red and gray fox, rat, mouse, bat, weasel, woodchuck, mink, muskrat, raccoon, beaver, rattlesnake, turtle, salamander, frog, toad

Birds: Ring-necked pheasant, Hungarian partridge, bobwhite, ruffed grouse, sharp-tailed grouse, mallard, teal, canvasback, redhead, widgeon duck, goose, loon, kingfisher, scarlet tanager, brown thrasher, warbler

Fish: Walleye and northern pike, Lake Superior cisco, whitefish, blue catfish, crappie, bullhead, carp, perch, sunfish, bluegill, rock sturgeon, largemouth and smallmouth bass, brook and rainbow trout

GOVERNMENT

Minnesota's prestatehood constitution, adopted in 1858, is still in effect, although more than a hundred amendments have been added over the years. Modeled after the U.S. Constitution, it calls for a three-part system of government.

The legislative branch consists of a 67-member senate and a 134-member house of representatives. Senators are elected to four-year terms; representatives, to two-year terms. Regular legislative sessions may meet no more than 120 days over two years, although the governor may call special sessions.

The executive branch includes the governor, lieutenant governor, secretary of state, auditor, treasurer, and attorney general. All are elected to four-year terms.

The governor also appoints the directors of many state boards and commissions. The terms of these positions vary from two to six years.

A supreme court, with a chief justice and eight associate justices, is the highest court in Minnesota's judicial branch. Members are elected to six-year terms. The state's court of appeals has twelve members who are elected to six-year terms. Minnesota's district court has ten judicial districts, each with three or more judges. County courts and municipal courts handle minor civil and criminal cases. The judges of these courts serve six-year terms.

Number of Counties: 87

U.S. Representatives: 8

Electoral Votes: 10

Voting Qualifications: Eighteen years of age; Minnesotans may register to vote on election day by presenting proper identification.

EDUCATION

Education has always been a top priority for Minnesotans. The state leads the nation in the percentage of students who complete high school. Minnesota's first schools date from the earliest settlement at Fort Snelling, and the territorial legislature created a public school system when Minnesota became a territory in 1849.

Today, Minnesota law requires that children between the ages of seven and sixteen attend school. Annual public school expenditures total about $4,000 per student, making the state eleventh in the nation in per capita school expenditures. Minnesota has many private schools, most of them Catholic or Lutheran parochial schools.

Minnesota also has extensive higher education, ranging from the huge, highly respected University of Minnesota, to some of the finest small private colleges in the country. The University of Minnesota has its main campus in the Twin Cities, and branch campuses in Duluth, Morris, Crookston, and Waseca. The Mayo Graduate School of Medicine, in Rochester, is also affiliated with the university. The Minnesota State University System operates universities in Winona, Marshall, Bemidji, St. Paul, Moorhead, St. Cloud, and Mankato, as well as fifteen junior colleges. Private schools include Augsburg College and Minneapolis College of Art and Design, both in Minneapolis; Bethel College, Bethel Theological Seminary, Hamline University, Luther Northwestern Theological Seminary, Macalester College, St. Paul Seminary School of Divinity, and College of St. Thomas, all in St. Paul; Carleton College and St. Olaf College, both in Northfield; Concordia College, in Moorhead; Dr. Martin Luther College, in New Ulm; Gustavus Adolphus College, in St. Peter; Northwestern College, in Roseville; College of St. Benedict, in St. Joseph; St. John's University, in Collegeville; St. Mary's College, in Winona; St. Paul Bible College, in Bible College; College of St. Scholastica, in Duluth; and United Theological Seminary, in New Brighton.

ECONOMY AND INDUSTRY

Principal Products:
Agriculture: Milk, soybeans, beef cattle, sheep, poultry, hogs, oats, corn, wheat, sugar beets, fruit, vegetables, barley, flax, hay, potatoes, berries
Manufacturing: Dairy products and other processed foods, lumber and forest products, office equipment and computers, electrical and nonelectrical machinery, transportation equipment, furniture, metal products, pulp and paper products, plastic products, stone, clay, and glass products
Natural Resources: Iron ore, granite, limestone, stone, clay, sand, gravel, wood, fish

Business: In its early years, Minnesota was on the western and northern edge of American settlement. Lumber and furs were the main industries. But Americans and foreign-born immigrants soon flocked to the rich farmlands and productive mines. Present-day Minnesota has one of the most balanced economies of any state, with healthy agriculture, mining, and manufacturing industries.

Grain farming and milling are important components of Minnesota's economy. Corn, soybeans, and hay are the most valuable crops. Minnesota ranks first in the nation in the production of sugar beets, and is among the leaders in hay, corn, soybeans, oats, barley, and rye. The nation's four largest flour mills are in Minneapolis. Livestock—mainly beef, hogs, and poultry—are another important part of farm income. Dairy cows grazing on central Minnesota farms helped earn the state the nickname Bread and Butter State.

Mining has long been a major industry in Minnesota. Minnesota leads the nation in iron-ore production, supplying more than two-thirds of the nation's total. The state also ranks high in production of limestone, granite, sand, and gravel.

Manufacturing is the leading component of Minnesota's economy. It includes agriculture-related businesses such as meat processing, dairy products, flour milling, and vegetable canning; electrical and nonelectrical machinery; fabricated metals; chemicals; lumber products; electronics; and computers.

Minnesota, because of its access to the Great Lakes, St. Lawrence Seaway, and Mississippi River, is the major marketing and distribution center of the upper Midwest. The Twin Cities area is a major rail, highway, and river trade center, as well as the financial center of the upper Midwest. Duluth is a major shipping center, particularly for iron ore and grain.

Communication: In 1849, James Madison Goodhue started publishing the *Minnesota Pioneer*, a newspaper that survives today as the *St. Paul Pioneer Press Dispatch*. It is the state's oldest newspaper. Today, Minnesota has about 30 daily and 290 weekly newspapers. Other important papers include the *Star Tribune* and the *Rochester Post-Bulletin*.

In 1922, WLB (now KUOM), a station owned by the University of Minnesota, became the state's first licensed radio station. The following year, Minneapolis's WDGY became Minnesota's first commercial station. Minnesota now has about 190 radio stations. In 1948, KSTP in Minneapolis became Minnesota's first television station. The state now has about 18 television stations.

Transportation: Minnesota is a land, water, and air transportation hub for the upper Midwest. The system of rivers and lakes provided movement for early explorers, fur traders, and missionaries. Even now, the Mississippi, Minnesota, and St. Croix rivers host extensive barge traffic. Duluth and nearby Superior, Wisconsin, share the busiest freshwater port in North America.

Railroads carry goods and people throughout the state to the rest of the continent. Minneapolis-St. Paul is the northernmost rail center of the Mississippi River Valley, and the most important one between the Great Lakes and the Pacific Coast. Minnesota has about 8,000 mi. (12,874 km) of railroad track. Twelve rail lines provide freight service, and passenger trains serve ten cities.

Highways now provide major transportation links for motorists and truckers. About 131,000 mi. (210,818 km) of roads cross the state. Interstate 94 runs east-west through the Twin Cities and across the state. Another important east-west highway, Interstate 90, cuts through southern Minnesota. Duluth is the northern origin of Interstate 35, a north-south highway that runs through the Midwest and Great Plains all the way to the Mexican border. Hibbing became the site of an important improvement in land transportation when the Greyhound Bus Company was founded there in 1914.

Northwest Airlines, one of the nation's largest carriers, has its corporate headquarters in Minnesota. Minnesota has 420 airports, of which 145 are publicly owned. The state's busiest airport is Minneapolis-St. Paul International Airport, which is served by eight major airlines.

SOCIAL AND CULTURAL LIFE

Museums: Minnesotans enjoy a wide variety of museums. The Minneapolis Institute of Arts is the largest art museum in the state. Others include the Walker Art Center in Minneapolis, which has a strong modern-art collection; University Gallery at the University of Minnesota; the Plains Art Museum in Moorhead, which features African, American Indian, and contemporary American exhibits; and the Minnesota Museum of Art in St. Paul.

The Minnesota Science Museum of St. Paul contains science, technology, and natural-history exhibits. In Duluth, the St. Louis County Heritage and Arts Center features a natural-history museum and historical society. Minneapolis boasts a planetarium that can project two thousand stars. The University of Minnesota in Minneapolis houses the James Ford Bell Museum of Natural History.

Minnesota also has a number of fine historical museums. St. Paul is the home of the Minnesota Historical Society Museum. The Lake Superior Museum of Transportation, in Duluth, exhibits railroad cars and equipment. Canal Park Marine Museum, also in Duluth, tells about commercial fishing in the upper Great Lakes. The Hinckley Fire Museum, in Hinckley, is an old railroad depot that commemorates the huge fire that ravaged the area in 1894.

Libraries: The University of Minnesota Library, with more than 3 million volumes, is the largest library in the state and one of the best research libraries in the nation. It houses large collections on children's literature, European expansion, and Scandinavia. The James J. Hill Reference Library, in St. Paul, is noted for its

Duluth's Lake Superior Museum of Transportation exhibits such historic trains as the *William Crooks*, Minnesota's first locomotive.

materials on the business and economics of the north-central states. The Mayo Foundation, in Rochester, houses an excellent medical library. Other special collections may be found at the State Law Library and the Minnesota Historical Society, both in St. Paul.

Minneapolis and St. Paul have the largest of the 330 public libraries in the state. Almost every community has a library. These are linked by an interlibrary system that is administered by the state department of education.

Performing Arts: The Tyrone Guthrie Theater in Minneapolis enjoys an outstanding national reputation. For more than twenty-five years, it has been considered one of the finest repertory theaters in the United States. Minneapolis's Children's Theatre Company is also nationally recognized. A number of smaller theater groups also flourish in the Twin Cities and on college campuses.

Music lovers may enjoy the Minneapolis-based Minnesota Symphony Orchestra or the St. Paul-based Minnesota Opera Company. Other musical organizations include the Schubert Club of St. Paul, the Apollo Club and Thursday Musical of Minneapolis, and the St. Olaf College Choir in Northfield. Other colleges and clubs throughout the state also provide music.

Sports and Recreation: Minnesota sports fans have a full choice of professional teams they can support: the Minnesota Twins, an American League baseball team; the Minnesota Vikings of the National Football League; the National Hockey League's Minnesota North Stars; and the recently formed Minnesota Timberwolves of the National Basketball Association. College fans may root for the Minnesota Gophers of the prestigious Big Ten Conference or for teams at many of the state's smaller colleges.

Minnesota, a haven for outdoor recreation, has sixty-four state parks and forty-five state forests. During the pleasant summers, thousands of Minnesotans take to the lakes and parks for camping, swimming, fishing, hiking, hunting, canoeing, tennis, or golf. Hearty souls willing to brave low winter temperatures enjoy skiing, tobogganing, ice fishing, and snowmobiling. In fact, the snowmobile was invented in Minnesota. Hockey is a mania in the state. Minnesota boasts more than two thousand amateur hockey teams, more than any other state. St. Paul celebrates the cold with a world-famous winter carnival.

Historic Sites and Landmarks:

Alexander Faribault House, in Faribault, was the home of one of Minnesota's early fur traders.

Freeborn County Historical Museum and Village, near Albert Lea, contains a restored schoolhouse, general store, sheriff's office and jail, blacksmith shop, wagon shops, train depot, church, and log cabin.

Grand Portage National Monument, in Grand Portage, preserves a former rendezvous point and supply depot of fur traders.

James J. Hill Mansion, in St. Paul, was the home of the famous Minnesota railroad magnate.

Historic Fort Snelling, near St. Paul, is a reconstruction of the 1820s frontier fortress.

Oliver H. Kelley Farm, near Elk River, is the family farm of the founder of the Grange movement.

Sinclair Lewis Home, in Sauk Centre, was the boyhood residence of America's first Nobel Prizewinning novelist.

Charles A. Lindbergh House and Interpretive Center, in Little Falls, was the boyhood home of the famous aviator and inventor.

W. W. Mayo House, in Le Sueur, is the restored 1859 home of William Mayo, who, with his sons, founded the world-famous Mayo Clinic.

Mayowood, in Rochester, is the fifty-five-room former home of Dr. Charles H. Mayo, son of W. W. Mayo and co-founder of the Mayo Clinic and the Mayo Foundation.

North West Company Fur Post, near Pine City, is a reconstruction of a nineteenth-century fur-trading outlet.

Northfield Bank Museum, in Northfield, commemorates an unsuccessful bank robbery attempt by Jesse James and his gang.

Pipestone National Monument, near Pipestone, is the site of a quarry that was visited for centuries by Indians who used its red stone to make ceremonial pipes.

Alexander Ramsey House, in St. Paul, is the splendid, 1872 French-Renaissance-style home of Alexander Ramsey, who served as Minnesota territorial governor, state governor, U.S. senator, and U.S. secretary of war.

Sibley House, in Mendota, was the residence of Minnesota's first state governor.

Other Interesting Places to Visit:

Agassiz National Wildlife Refuge, near Thief River Falls, covers more than 60,000 acres (more than 24,000 hectares) and provides a haven for 245 species of migratory and game birds.

Paul Bunyan and Babe Statues, in Bemidji, are giant likenesses of the legendary Minnesota lumberjack and his blue ox.

Eloise Butler Wildflower Garden and Bird Sanctuary, in Minneapolis, contains a natural bog, swamp, and habitat for prairie flowers and birds.

Glensheen, in Duluth, is the unique and impressive estate of mining mogul Chester A. Congdon. Built in 1905, it reflects the elegant way of life that existed in Duluth at that time.

Glockenspiel, in New Ulm, is a 45-ft.- (14-m-) high musical clock tower with animated performing figures.

Hull-Rust Mahoning Mine, near Hibbing, allows visitors to view the "Grand Canyon of Minnesota," a mine that is 3 mi. (5 km) long and 535 ft. (163 m) deep.

Indian Mounds Park, in St. Paul, contains mounds that were used as grave sites or places of worship by mound-building Indians.

International Falls, has a 22-ft.- (7-m-) high thermometer that displays the town's icy winter temperatures.

The Iron Man Memorial stands near the entrance of Ironworld USA, which celebrates the heritage of Minnesota's iron-range region.

Ironworld USA, in Chisholm, which explores the history of mining in Minnesota, features the Iron Range Interpretative Center, a tour of an open-pit mine, and an outdoor amphitheater.

Itasca State Park, near Park Rapids, is the site of the source of the Mississippi River.

Kensington Runestone, in Alexander, contains inscriptions believed to date from a Viking exploration to the Minnesota area in 1362.

Lumbertown U.S.A., near Brainerd, is a replica of an old-time lumber town with more than thirty buildings.

Mayo Clinic, in Rochester, is a world-famous medical center that serves more than 250,000 patients per year.

Minnehaha Falls, in Minneapolis, is the "laughing water" of the epic poem *Hiawatha*.

Nicollet Mall, in Minneapolis, is a famous pedestrian shopping mall complete with museums, restaurants, art galleries and shops connected by enclosed skyways.

Smokey Bear Park, in International Falls, displays logging equipment, toys, and tools, and honors the symbol of forest-fire prevention with a statue.

State Capitol, in St. Paul, completed in 1905, contains one of the largest self-supporting marble domes in the world.

Sugar Loaf, in Winona, is an unusual limestone formation atop a 500-ft. (152-m) bluff.

United States Hockey Hall of Fame, in Eveleth, honors American hockey and its players.

University of Minnesota, in Minneapolis, is the largest single college campus in the United States.

IMPORTANT DATES

c. 20,000 B.C.—Humans first roam the lands that are now Minnesota

c. 10,000 B.C.—Last glacier retreats from present-day Minnesota

c. 4000 B.C.—Copper culture begins in Minnesota

c. 500 B.C.—Mound-building Indian civilization thrives in Minnesota

c. A.D. 1659—French traders Pierre Radisson and Médard Chouart, Sieur des Groseilliers, become the first known white men to visit Minnesota

1679—Daniel Greysolon, Sieur Duluth, explores northeastern and eastern Minnesota

1680—Father Louis Hennepin, a Belgian missionary, explores the upper Mississippi River Valley and is captured by Dakota Indians

1689—Nicolas Perrot builds a fort on Lake Pepin

1731—Pierre Gautier de Varennes, Sieur de La Vérendrye, discovers a canoe route for the fur trade from Lake Superior to Lake of the Woods

1763—Britain takes Minnesota from France following the French and Indian War; Great Lakes Indians rebel and attack British forts

1783—Treaty of Paris, ending the Revolutionary War, gives eastern Minnesota to the U.S.

1803 — Louisiana Purchase gives the rest of Minnesota to the U.S.

1805 — Zebulon Pike explores Minnesota to select fort sites

1819 — Construction of Fort St. Anthony (later named Fort Snelling) begins

1820 — First school for white children in the Minnesota region opens at Fort St. Anthony

1825 — An Indian treaty gives the rest of present-day Minnesota to the Dakota and Ojibwa

1832 — Henry R. Schoolcraft discovers Lake Itasca, source of the Mississippi River

1837 — U.S. government purchases land between St. Croix and Mississippi rivers from the Ojibwa

1841 — Father Lucian Galtier builds a Catholic chapel that becomes the center of present-day St. Paul

1847 — Settlement begins at the Falls of St. Anthony, which later becomes Minneapolis

1849 — Congress creates the Minnesota Territory; the *Minnesota Pioneer,* the state's first newspaper, begins publication

1851 — Territorial legislature establishes the College of Liberal Arts, which later becomes the University of Minnesota; the Dakota cede 28 million acres (11 million hectares) of southern Minnesota lands

1854 — A treaty with the Ojibwa gives Minnesota claim to rich timberland in northern Minnesota

1857 — The Minnesota Constitutional Convention adopts a state constitution

1858 — Minnesota joins the Union as the thirty-second state

1861 — Minnesota becomes the first state to volunteer troops for the Union army in the Civil War

1862 — Troops subdue a Dakota uprising known as the Dakota War; Homestead Act offers free land to settlers and causes a population boom; the first railroad in Minnesota begins running from St. Paul to St. Anthony (now Minneapolis)

1865 — Geologist H. H. Eames discovers iron deposits in Vermilion Range

1868 — The Grange movement begins when Minnesotan Oliver H. Kelley begins organizing local granges (farmers' cooperative associations) in Minnesota

1873 — A great blizzard kills at least seventy people in Minnesota

1876 — Bank officials and law officers in Northfield foil a bank robbery attempt by famed outlaw Jesse James and his gang

1878 — Three Minneapolis flour mills explode, killing eighteen people

1884 — The first shipment of iron ore from the Vermilion Range is shipped from the state

1889 — The Mayo family founds the clinic that bears their name, in Rochester

1890 — The Merritt family discovers the nation's largest iron-ore deposits, in the Mesabi Range

1894 — A fire destroys 400 sq. mi. (1,036 km^2) of timber, kills 418 persons, and destroys the towns of Hinckley and Sandstone

1905 — Present State Capitol is completed

1922 — WLB, the state's first radio station, begins broadcasting

1927 — Minnesotan Charles Lindbergh, Jr., becomes the first person to make a solo, nonstop flight across the Atlantic Ocean

1929 — Minnesotan Frank Billings Kellogg wins the Nobel Peace Prize for negotiating the Kellogg-Briand Pact, which denounced war as a means of foreign policy

1930 — Minnesotan Sinclair Lewis becomes the first American to win the Nobel Prize for literature

1931 — Minnesota becomes one of the first states to establish a department of conservation

1944 — The state Democratic and Farmer-Labor political parties unite

1948 — Hubert Humphrey, young mayor of Minneapolis, adds an important civil-rights plank to the Democratic party platform and is elected to the U.S. Senate; Harold Stassen makes his first campaign for the Republican presidential nomination

1950 — Minnesotan Philip S. Hench wins the Nobel Prize for medicine for his use of hormones to treat rheumatoid arthritis

1955 — Taconite processing begins at Silver Bay on Lake Superior

1960 — Hubert Humphrey runs a spirited race but loses Democratic nomination for the presidency

1961 — Minnesotan Melvin Calvin wins the Nobel Prize for chemistry for his work with photosynthesis

1963 — The Tyrone Guthrie Theater, now one of the most acclaimed theaters in America, opens

1964 — President Lyndon B. Johnson selects Hubert Humphrey as his vice-presidential running mate; they win in a landslide election; Minnesota voters approve the Taconite Amendment

1968 — Vice-President Humphrey loses a close presidential election to Richard Nixon

1970 — Congress creates Voyageurs National Park, the first national park in Minnesota

1972 — A government reorganization consolidates state agencies

1975 — Minnesota's Republican party changes its name to Independent-Republicans of Minnesota

1976 — Presidential nominee Jimmy Carter chooses Minnesotan Walter Mondale for vice-president, and the Carter-Mondale team wins a close presidential election

1982 — A state constitutional amendment establishes a court of appeals

1984 — Democratic presidential candidate Walter Mondale loses in a landslide to Republican Ronald Reagan, though he carries his home state of Minnesota

1987 — The Minnesota Twins win the World Series, the state's first national sports championship in more than thirty years

EUGENIE ANDERSON

THE ANDREWS SISTERS

PATTY BERG

WARREN BURGER

IMPORTANT PEOPLE

Eugenie M. Anderson (1909-   ), politician, diplomat; an architect of Minnesota's Democratic-Farmer-Labor party; first American woman ambassador; represented the U.S. in Denmark and Bulgaria, and as U.S. representative on the United Nations Trusteeship Council

La Verne (1916-1967), **Maxene** (1918-   ), and **Patti** (1920-   ) **Andrews**, all born in Minneapolis; singers; entertained U.S. troops and Americans during World War II as the Andrews Sisters; famous songs included "Rum and Cola" and "Boogie Woogie Bugle Boy of Company B"

James Arness (1923-   ), born in Minneapolis; actor; starred for many years as sheriff Matt Dillon in the television western "Gunsmoke"

Lew Ayres (1908-   ), born in Minneapolis; actor; best known for portraying the character Dr. Kildare in a series of films; other films included *Advise and Consent* and *All Quiet on the Western Front*

Charles Albert (Chief) Bender (1884-1954), born in Crow Wing County; professional baseball player; Chippewa Indian who starred as pitcher for Philadelphia Athletics; led his team to five pennants and three world championships; won six World Series games; elected to Baseball Hall of Fame (1953)

Patty Berg (1918-   ), born Patricia June Berry in Minneapolis; professional golfer; won 1938 U.S. Women's Amateur championship and 1946 U.S. Women's Open championship

Harry Andrew Blackmun (1908-   ), lawyer, judge; worked as a lawyer in Minneapolis and Rochester; served in Minnesota as judge of Eighth Circuit of U.S. Court of Appeals (1959-70); U.S. Supreme Court associate justice (1970-   )

Robert Elwood Bly (1926-   ), born in Madison; poet; won National Book Award in poetry (1968); best-known books include *Silence in the Snowy Fields* and *The Morning Glory*

Rudolph (Rudy) Boschwitz (1930-   ), businessman, politician; founder of Plywood Minnesota, a do-it-yourself building materials chain; U.S. senator from Minnesota (1979-   ); specializes in refugee issues, as he himself was a refugee from Nazi Germany

Warren Earl Burger (1907-   ), born in St. Paul; lawyer, judge; U.S. Supreme Court chief justice (1969-86); presided over decisions allowing the use of school busing to achieve integration, easing restrictions on police and prosecuting attorneys, and upholding the use of capital punishment

Pierce Butler (1866-1939), born in Dakota County; judge; U.S. Supreme Court associate justice (1922-39); had conservative sympathies; voted to uphold government restrictions on civil liberties

Melvin Calvin (1911-   ), born in St. Paul; chemist; won 1961 Nobel Prize in chemistry for his work with photosynthesis

Gino Cappaletti (1934-   ), born in Keewatin; professional football player; kicked field goals and extra points for Boston (now New England) Patriots; led American Football League (now American Football Conference) in scoring during three seasons

Tony Charmoli (1922-   ), born in Minneapolis; choreographer; directed dance sequences for television variety shows starring Julie Andrews, Cher, Dinah Shore, Danny Kaye, and Jonathan Winters; won several Emmy awards

Arlene Dahl (1928-   ), born in Minneapolis; actress, writer; wrote an internationally syndicated beauty column; appeared in Broadway plays, films, and television

Richard Dix (1894-1949), born Ernest Brimmer in St. Paul; actor; became one of America's leading heroes during the silent movie era; starred in *Cimarron*

Ignatius Donnelly (1831-1901), writer, politician; U.S. representative from Minnesota (1863-69); helped form the Populist party (1891); supported a federal income tax, government ownership of railroads, and an eight-hour workday

William Orville Douglas (1898-1980), born in Maine, Minnesota; teacher, lawyer, judge; U.S. Supreme Court associate justice (1939-75); served longer than any other justice in American history; believed in a strong interpretation of the Bill of Rights; was considered one of the greatest justices in Supreme Court history; led fights for conservation and freedom of speech

Daniel Greysolon, Sieur Duluth (1636-1710), explorer; traveled through the northern Lake Superior region, including the land that would become the city that bears his name

David Durenberger (1934-   ), born in St. Cloud; politician; U.S. senator from Minnesota (1978-   ); chaired the Senate Intelligence Committee (1985, 1986); used his position to oppose aid to the Nicaraguan contra forces

Bob Dylan (1941-   ), born Robert Zimmerman in Duluth; musician, composer; influenced a generation of musicians as a folk, rock, and country music writer; wrote many famous songs, including ''Blowin' in the Wind,'' ''The Times They Are A-Changin','' and ''Like a Rolling Stone''

Mike Farrell (1942-   ), born in St. Paul; actor, director; portrayed Dr. B. J. Honeycutt in the famed television series ''M*A*S*H''

MELVIN CALVIN

TONY CHARMOLI

IGNATIUS DONNELLY

WILLIAM O. DOUGLAS

ORVILLE FREEMAN

JUDY GARLAND

J. PAUL GETTY

CASS GILBERT

Francis Scott (F. Scott) Fitzgerald (1896-1940), born in St. Paul; writer; one of the leading American writers of the twentieth century; portrayed free-living high-society life in the Roaring Twenties in such books as *The Great Gatsby, Tender Is the Night,* and *The Last Tycoon*

Ed Flanders (1934-   ), born in Minneapolis; actor; performed at the Guthrie Theater in the 1960s; winner of three Emmy awards, including a 1983 award for his portrayal of Dr. Donald Westphal on the television series "St. Elsewhere"

William Watts Folwell (1833-1929), educator, historian; first president of the University of Minnesota (1869-84); led a campaign to develop junior colleges in the state; wrote *A History of Minnesota*

Orville Freeman (1918-   ), born in Minneapolis; statesman; governor of Minnesota (1955-61); U.S. secretary of agriculture (1961-69) under Presidents John F. Kennedy and Lyndon B. Johnson

Judy Garland (1922-1969), born Frances Gumm in Grand Rapids; actress, singer; delighted millions as Dorothy in *The Wizard of Oz;* other well-known films include *Meet Me in St. Louis* and *A Star Is Born*

Jean Paul (J. Paul) Getty (1892-1976), born in Minneapolis; businessman; earned $4 billion in the oil business, making him one of the wealthiest men in the world; wrote *History of the Oil Business of George F. and J. Paul Getty*

Cass Gilbert (1859-1934), architect; helped begin a Classical revival in American architecture with such public buildings as the State Capitol in St. Paul and the University of Minnesota campus in Minneapolis

Philip Showalter Hench (1896-1965), physician; worked at the Mayo Clinic (1923-57); co-winner of 1950 Nobel Prize in physiology or medicine for his use of hormones in treating rheumatoid arthritis

Louis Hennepin (1626?-1701), missionary, explorer; traveled the upper Mississippi River before being captured by Dakota Indians; sighted and named the Falls of St. Anthony, which would become the site of Minneapolis

James Jerome Hill (1838-1916), businessman; founded Great Northern Railway, which linked the Great Lakes to the Pacific Coast; became known as the "Empire Builder"; founded a steamship line that offered the first direct service from the United States to the Orient

Kent Allen Hrbek (1960-   ), born in Minneapolis; professional baseball player; All-Star first baseman with the Minnesota Twins; hit a grand-slam home run that helped lead the Twins to the 1987 World Series championship

Hubert Horatio Humphrey (1911-1978), politician; mayor of Minneapolis (1945-48); helped merge Minnesota's Democratic and Farmer-Labor parties in 1944; U.S. senator from Minnesota (1949-65, 1971-78); U.S. vice-president under Lyndon Johnson (1965-69); lost the presidential election to Richard Nixon in 1968; as a U.S. senator, became a champion of civil rights and humanitarian issues

John Ireland (1838-1918), religious leader; bishop (1884-88) and first archbishop (1888-1918) of St. Paul; led temperance movement; organized the Catholic Colonization Bureau to bring poor Irish immigrants from eastern slums to Midwest farms; helped found Catholic University in Washington, D.C. (1889)

Garrison Keillor (1942-   ), born in Anoka; humorist, writer; entertained millions with his gentle country humor as host of public radio's "A Prairie Home Companion"

Oliver Hudson Kelley (1826-1913), agrarian reformer; started the Grange movement when, in 1868, he began organizing local farmers' groups in Minnesota; founded the Patrons of Husbandry (or National Grange), the first farm organization in the United States

Frank Billings Kellogg (1856-1937), lawyer, politician, diplomat; U.S. senator from Minnesota (1917-23); ambassador to Great Britain (1923-25); U.S. secretary of state (1925-29); formulated the Kellogg-Briand Pact, an attempt to outlaw war (1928); won the Nobel Peace Prize in 1929

Elizabeth Kenny (1880-1952), known as Sister Kenny; Australian nurse who developed a method of rehabilitating polio patients; came to the U.S. and set up the Elizabeth Kenny Institute in Minneapolis (1940)

Jessica Lange (1949-   ), grew up in Minnesota; actress; starred in such films as *The Postman Always Rings Twice, Frances,* and *The Music Box*; several-time Academy Award nominee

Sinclair Lewis (1885-1951), born in Sauk Centre; writer; portrayed and often satirized small-town life in such books as *Main Street, Arrowsmith, Babbitt,* and *Elmer Gantry*; won but declined the Pulitzer Prize in fiction in 1926 (for *Arrowsmith*); first American to win the Nobel Prize in literature (1930)

Charles Augustus Lindbergh, Jr. (1902-1974), aviator; grew up in Little Falls; made the first nonstop solo flight across the Atlantic Ocean; wrote the book *We* about his flight

Little Crow (1820?-1863), Dakota Indian chief; signed treaties opening southeastern Minnesota to white settlement (1851); tried to maintain peace with whites in spite of mounting grievances against them; though he was against attacking the white settlers, he stood by his people and led Dakota forces during the Dakota War of 1862

OLIVER KELLEY

FRANK KELLOGG

ELIZABETH KENNY

LITTLE CROW

PAUL MANSHIP

ROGER MARIS

EUGENE McCARTHY

LAURIS NORSTAD

Cornell MacNeil (1922-   ), born in Minneapolis; opera singer, labor official; became known as one of the great baritone interpreters of Giuseppe Verdi; sang in *Aida* and *Nabucco*; led the American Guild of Musical Artists

Paul Manship (1885-1966), born in St. Paul; sculptor; sculpted in a classical style; sculpted the Prometheus Fountain at Rockefeller Center in New York City

Roger Maris (1934-1985), born in Hibbing; professional baseball player; holds major league record for most home runs in one season (61, in 1961); won American League Most Valuable Player award in 1960 and 1961

E. G. Marshall (1910-   ), born in Owatonna; actor; starred in many programs during the "Golden Age" of television drama; played a lawyer in the acclaimed series "The Defenders"; winner of two Emmy awards

Charles Horace Mayo (1861-1939), born in Le Sueur, and **William James Mayo** (1865-1939), born in Rochester; physicians; with their father, W. W. Mayo, founded the Mayo Clinic in Rochester, today one of the world's largest and most famous medical centers; through the Mayo Clinic, pioneered the concept of a cooperative group clinic; donated $1.5 million in 1915 to establish the Mayo Foundation; founded the Mayo Graduate School of Medicine

William Worrall Mayo (1819-1911), physician; helped organize Minnesota Territory; served as U.S. Army surgeon during 1862 Dakota War; with his sons, helped Sisters of St. Francis found St. Mary's Hospital in Rochester (1889), which led to the formation of the Mayo Clinic

Eugene McCarthy (1916-   ), born in Watkins; politician; U.S. representative from Minnesota (1949-59); U.S. senator (1959-71); as a senator, was an outspoken critic of the Vietnam War

Walter Frederick "Fritz" Mondale (1928-   ), born in Ceylon; politician; U.S. senator from Minnesota (1964-77); became known for his liberal views; U.S. vice-president under Jimmy Carter (1977-81); won Democratic nomination for president in 1984, but lost to Ronald Reagan; first major-party American presidential candidate to choose a woman (Geraldine Ferraro) as his running mate

Lauris Norstad (1907-1988), born in Minneapolis; military officer; served as Supreme Allied Commander of NATO forces (1956-63)

Eugene Ormandy (1899-1985), conductor; directed the Minneapolis Symphony Orchestra (1931-36); helped the symphony gain a reputation as "Minnesota's outstanding contribution to the world of music"; later directed the Philadelphia Orchestra (1936-80)

Zebulon Montgomery Pike (1779-1813), army officer, explorer; led an expedition (1805) that suggested sites for forts in the Upper Mississippi Valley

John Sargent Pillsbury (1828-1901), politician, businessman; governor of Minnesota (1876-82); favored measures to benefit agriculture and education in Minnesota; became known as the "Father of the University of Minnesota"

Alexander Ramsey (1815-1903), politician; first territorial governor of Minnesota (1849-53); state governor (1860-63); secured lands from the Dakota and Ojibwa that opened up the Minnesota Territory for white settlement; U.S. senator from Minnesota (1863-75); U.S. secretary of war (1879-81)

Henry Mower Rice (1816-1894), politician; helped arrange treaties that enabled Minnesota to gain Indian lands; U.S. senator from Minnesota (1858-63)

Ole Edvart Rolvaag (1876-1931), educator, writer; professor of Norwegian at St. Olaf College (1906-31); wrote *Giants in the Earth*, which described the harsh life of the Minnesota pioneers

Jane Russell (1921-), born in Bemidji; actress; starred in many films, including *The Outlaw* and *Gentlemen Prefer Blondes*

Charles M. Schulz (1922-), born in Minneapolis; cartoonist; created the funny but philosophical comic strip "Peanuts," which features such famous characters as Charlie Brown, Snoopy, and Linus

Richard Warren Sears (1863-1914), born in Stewartville; merchant, businessman; with A. C. Roebuck, started the Sears Roebuck mail order company, which became the world's largest retailer (1890); moved the business to Chicago in 1893

Max Shulman (1919-), born in St. Paul; humorist; wrote of life in middle America in such plays as *Rally Round the Flag, Boys*; wrote the television series "Dobie Gillis"

Henry Hastings Sibley (1811-1891), politician; presided over Democratic branch of Minnesota's state constitutional convention (1857); first Minnesota state governor (1858-60); commanded troops that suppressed an 1862 Dakota uprising

Harold Stassen (1907-), born in St. Paul; politician; governor of Minnesota (1939-43); as governor, revised civil-service laws and lowered government costs

Jane Grey Swisshelm (1815-1884), publisher, social reformer; Minnesota's most famous newspaperwoman; founded the *St. Cloud Visiter*, in which she published editorials denouncing slavery; wrote about and lectured on the issue of women's rights

Lawrence Taliaferro (1794-1871), Indian agent; managed the fur trade, issued licenses, and protected the interests and welfare of the Indians; strove to maintain peace between the Dakota and Ojibwa

JOHN PILLSBURY

ALEXANDER RAMSEY

JANE RUSSELL

RICHARD SEARS

DEWITT WALLACE

RICHARD WIDMARK

Thorstein Veblen (1857-1929), economist, sociologist; graduated from Carleton College; analyzed American consumerism in his book *The Theory of the Leisure Class*

William Roy DeWitt Wallace (1899-1981), born in St. Paul; editor, publisher; founded and published *Reader's Digest*, the world's largest-selling magazine

Richard Widmark (1915-   ), born in Sunrise; actor; portrayed heroes with a barely suppressed sense of violence; starred in many films, including *Kiss of Death* and *Judgment at Nuremberg*

Roy Wilkins (1901-1981), civil rights leader; grew up in St. Paul and graduated from the University of Minnesota; leader in the fight for equal rights for blacks; executive director of the National Association for the Advancement of Colored People (NAACP)

David Mark (Dave) Winfield (1951-   ), born in St. Paul; professional baseball player; was such a fine athlete at the University of Minnesota that he was drafted by professional baseball, football, and basketball teams; led National League in runs batted in for 1979 season

Gig Young (1917-1978), born Byron Barr in St. Cloud; actor; starred as a likeable con man in the television show "The Rogues"; performed in many television programs during the 1950s "Golden Age" of television drama

GOVERNORS

Henry H. Sibley	1858-1860	Theodore Christianson	1925-1931
Alexander Ramsey	1860-1863	Floyd B. Olson	1931-1936
Henry A. Swift	1863-1864	Hjalmar Petersen	1936-1937
Stephen Miller	1864-1866	Elmer A. Benson	1937-1939
William R. Marshall	1866-1870	Harold E. Stassen	1939-1943
Horace Austin	1870-1874	Edward J. Thye	1943-1947
Cushman K. Davis	1874-1876	Luther W. Youngdahl	1947-1951
John S. Pillsbury	1876-1882	C. Elmer Anderson	1951-1955
Lucius F. Hubbard	1882-1887	Orville L. Freeman	1955-1961
Andrew R. McGill	1887-1889	Elmer L. Anderson	1961-1963
William R. Merriam	1889-1893	Karl F. Rolvaag	1963-1967
Knute Nelson	1893-1895	Harold E. LeVander	1967-1971
David M. Clough	1895-1899	Wendell R. Anderson	1971-1976
John Lind	1899-1901	Rudolph G. Perpich	1976-1979
Samuel R. Van Sant	1901-1905	Albert H. Quie	1979-1983
John A. Johnson	1905-1909	Rudolph G. Perpich	1983-
Adolph O. Eberhart	1909-1915		
Winfield S. Hammond	1915		
Joseph A. A. Burnquist	1915-1921		
Jacob A. O. Preus	1921-1925		

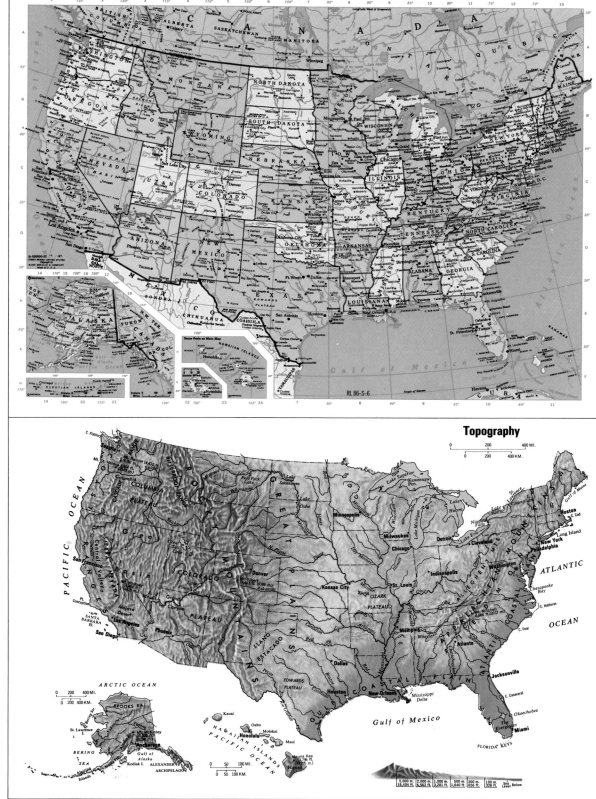

Topography

MAP KEY

MANITOBA

ONTARIO

CANADA
U.S.

NORTH DAKOTA

SOUTH DAKOTA

WISCONSIN

IOWA

Lake of the Woods

RED LAKE INDIAN RES.

VOYAGEURS NATIONAL PARK

LEECH LAKE INDIAN RES.

WHITE EARTH INDIAN RESERVATION

MILLE LACS IND. RES.

FOND DU LAC IND. RES.

Lake Superior

Grand Forks

Fargo

Moorhead

Thief River Falls

Bemidji

Grand Rapids

Virginia

Hibbing

Duluth

Superior

Fergus Falls

Alexandria

Brainerd

Little Falls

St. Cloud

Willmar

Hutchinson

Minneapolis

St. Paul

Mankato

New Ulm

Marshall

Worthington

Fairmont

Albert Lea

Austin

Rochester

Winona

La Crosse

Red Wing

Faribault

Northfield

Owatonna

Brookings

Sioux Falls

Watertown

Milbank

Ashland

Two Harbors

International Falls

Fort Frances

Grand Marais

EAGLE MTN. – 2301 HIGHEST PT. IN MINN.

ONT. MINN.

GRAND PORTAGE IND. RES.

Same Scale as Main Map

Lake Superior

St. Michael

Brooklyn Park

Minnetonka

Bloomington

Edina

Richfield

Eagan

Apple Valley

Burnsville

Shakopee

Chaska

Chanhassen

Minneapolis

St. Paul

Statute Miles

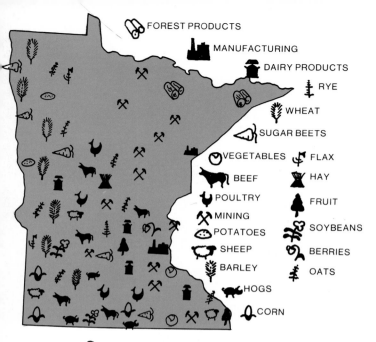

FOREST PRODUCTS
MANUFACTURING
DAIRY PRODUCTS
RYE
WHEAT
SUGAR BEETS
VEGETABLES   FLAX
BEEF   HAY
POULTRY   FRUIT
MINING
POTATOES   SOYBEANS
SHEEP   BERRIES
BARLEY   OATS
HOGS
CORN

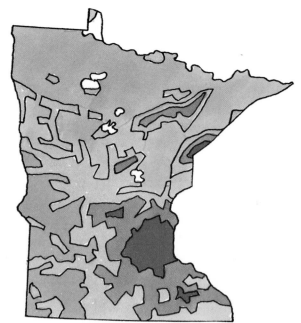

POPULATION DENSITY

Number of persons per square kilometer		Number of persons per square mile
more than 40		more than 100
20 to 40		50 to 100
10 to 20		25 to 50
Less than 10		Less than 25

MAJOR HIGHWAYS

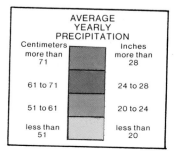

AVERAGE YEARLY PRECIPITATION

Centimeters		Inches
more than 71		more than 28
61 to 71		24 to 28
51 to 61		20 to 24
less than 51		less than 20

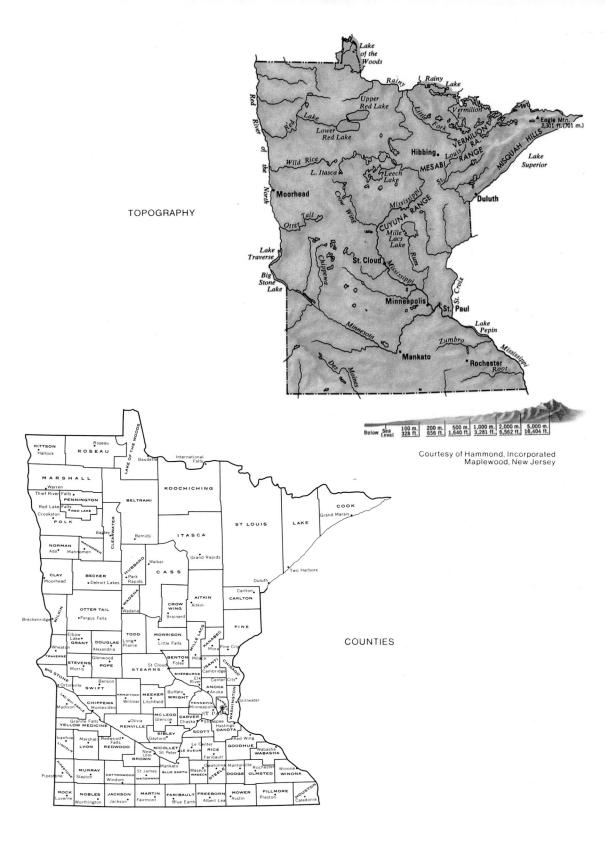

TOPOGRAPHY

Eagle Mtn.
2,301 ft. (701 m.)

Lake of the Woods

Rainy
Rainy Lake
Vermilion
Little Fork

Upper Red Lake
Red Lake
Lower Red Lake

VERMILION RA. RANGE
MISQUAH HILLS
Lake Superior

Hibbing
MESABI
Louis

Wild Rice
L. Itasca
Leech Lake

St.

Moorhead
Crow Wing
CUYUNA RANGE
Duluth

Mississippi

Mille Lacs Lake
St. Cloud
Rum
Mississippi

Otter Tail

Chippewa

Lake Traverse

Big Stone Lake

Minneapolis
St. Paul
St. Croix

Minnesota
Lake Pepin

Mankato
Zumbro
Mississippi
Des Moines
Rochester
Root

Below Sea Level | 100 m. 328 ft. | 200 m. 656 ft. | 500 m. 1,640 ft. | 1,000 m. 3,281 ft. | 2,000 m. 6,562 ft. | 5,000 m. 16,404 ft.

Courtesy of Hammond, Incorporated
Maplewood, New Jersey

COUNTIES

KITTSON
Hallock

Roseau
ROSEAU

LAKE OF THE WOODS
Baudette

International Falls

MARSHALL
Warren

PENNINGTON
Thief River Falls

Red Lake Falls
RED LAKE
Crookston

BELTRAMI

KOOCHICHING

ST LOUIS

COOK
Grand Marais

LAKE

POLK
Bagley
CLEARWATER
Bemidji

ITASCA
Grand Rapids

NORMAN
Ada
MAHNOMEN
Mahnomen

HUBBARD
Park Rapids
Walker

CASS

Duluth
Two Harbors

CLAY
Moorhead

BECKER
Detroit Lakes

WADENA
Wadena

CROW WING
Brainerd

AITKIN
Aitkin

CARLTON
Carlton

WILKIN
Breckenridge

OTTER TAIL
Fergus Falls

TODD
Long Prairie

MORRISON
Little Falls

MILLE LACS

PINE

Elbow Lake
GRANT

DOUGLAS
Alexandria

KANABEC
Mora
Pine City

TRAVERSE
Wheaton

STEVENS
Morris
Glenwood
POPE

STEARNS
St Cloud
Foley
BENTON

SHERBURNE
Elk River

ISANTI
Cambridge

CHISAGO
Center City

BIG STONE
Ortonville

SWIFT
Benson

MEEKER
Litchfield

WRIGHT
Buffalo

ANOKA
Anoka

Stillwater

LAC QUI PARLE
Madison

CHIPPEWA
Montevideo

KANDIYOHI
Willmar

HENNEPIN
Minneapolis
WASHINGTON

YELLOW MEDICINE
Granite Falls

RENVILLE
Olivia

McLEOD
Glencoe

CARVER
Chaska

Shakopee
SCOTT
Hastings
DAKOTA

Red Wing

Ivanhoe
LINCOLN

Marshall
LYON

Redwood Falls
REDWOOD

SIBLEY
Gaylord

NICOLLET
St Peter

LE SUEUR
Le Center

RICE
Faribault

GOODHUE

WABASHA
Wabasha

PIPESTONE
Pipestone

MURRAY
Slayton

COTTONWOOD
Windom

BROWN
New Ulm

BLUE EARTH
Mankato

WATONWAN
St James

WASECA
Waseca

STEELE
Owatonna

DODGE
Mantorville

OLMSTED
Rochester

WINONA
Winona

ROCK
Luverne

NOBLES
Worthington

JACKSON
Jackson

MARTIN
Fairmont

FARIBAULT
Blue Earth

FREEBORN
Albert Lea

MOWER
Austin

FILLMORE
Preston

HOUSTON
Caledonia

A winter scene along Lake Superior

INDEX

Page numbers that appear in boldface type indicate illustrations

A boy enjoying fresh corn at the Minnesota State Fair in St. Paul

Picture Identifications
Front cover: The Minneapolis skyline at night
Back cover: View of Palisade Head jutting into Lake Superior along North Shore Drive near Silver Bay
Pages 2-3: Split Rock Lighthouse on the North Shore
Page 6: Autumn at Split Rock Lighthouse State Park
Pages 8-9: The Temperance River in winter
Pages 20-21: Montage of Minnesota residents
Page 26: Indian artifacts displayed at Pipestone National Monument
Pages 40-41: An 1890 photograph showing miners at the Tower-Soudan Mine
Page 56: Minneapolis Mayor Hubert Humphrey championing a civil rights platform at the 1948 Democratic National Convention
Page 68: The Minnesota State Capitol in St. Paul
Pages 76-77: An ice palace at the St. Paul Winter Carnival
Pages 90-91: Minneapolis at dusk
Page 108: Montage showing the state flag, state tree (red pine), state flower (showy lady's-slipper), state gemstone (Lake Superior agate), and state fish (walleye)

About the Author

R. Conrad Stein was born and grew up in Chicago. He received a degree in history from the University of Illinois, and later studied at the University of Guanajuato in Mexico. He is the author of many books, articles, and short stories written for young readers. Mr. Stein lives in Chicago with his wife and their daughter Janna.